DRAWING FIRE

Vietnam Through the Eyes of a Combat Artist

Ed Bowen

WINEPRESS WP PUBLISHING

ISBN 1-57921-300-6
Library of Congress Catalog Card Number: 00-102415

CONTENTS

Introduction

"Kill, kill, kill," I yelled as I thrust a bayonet into a dummy that my drill sergeant had nicknamed Charley. "Yell louder, Bowen, like you mean it!"

No, no, no, I thought, because I didn't hate Charley. But, I yelled louder, as was demanded. I had to. I had no choice. As part of the war machine, I had to do my part. Over and over again I yelled, "Kill, kill, kill!" as ordered—with meaning too—even though, inside, I faked the meaning. The sergeant finally let up, when he figured I was a kindred spirit. It was a cover-up.

The wheels turning in my mind asked why I should be killing Charley. What has he done to me? There were two different wars going on: the one that was out to do evil and then mine, the one that was out to do good. There may be more to this than I had thought, however. Maybe the war protesters were telling the truth—that greed is the bottom line in this war. Profiteers are getting rich, I heard; and maybe it is true that we are supporting a corrupt South Vietnamese government.

What about communism, though? Isn't it a corrupt form of government, out to control all of Asia? Shouldn't we help those who don't want a communistic rule? Should we kill to stop that? Question, questions, questions filled my head in searching for the answer to why I should, or could, agree with the orders to kill Charley. Less than five years earlier, when I was a college freshman, I didn't have to answer these questions. Back then I was asking, "Where will my education take me?"

Stabbing at the dummy, I thought, *A month earlier, I had high school kids asking me questions as they addressed their instructor, Mr. Bowen.*

What an abrupt change from a life of somewhat comfortable ease to one that demanded such intense dedication to something so nebulous and undefined. I wasn't the only one with this concern; thousands searched their hearts for conviction that would carry them through this ordeal.

Many had their own way of coping, like running to Canada, protesting against their government, or supporting their country and government in cause, and even entering the war itself.

"Please, Mr. Custer, I Don't Wanna Go" was the popular song of a soldier who was forced to enter a sure-lose battle against the Indians. The man, in history, did go to battle and did perish—no one who followed him survived. Young men didn't want to go to Vietnam either. They sang, "Please, Mr. Johnson, I don't want to go." A point was to have been made; everyone tried, but no point was made, in the end. The dedicated, being loyal, were mostly kindhearted—not wanting to kill—but entered the service with vigor. How many times did I witness their tears of anguish that broke my heart. One of the most profound pictures still lingers in my mind. One of these fellows, with tears in his eyes, looked at me and said, "I can't stand the thought of never seeing my wife again." This was the last time I saw him, a door gunner. I am not certain if his wife ever saw his name on the Nam wall in Washington, D.C.

Looking back, I can see that each had his personal emotion tied to this war; each had his own story. But there were stories so bitter that words could not seep from some mouths because of the emotional damage of battle—too cruel to think, without a breakdown. The most profound stories were silenced by a long marble wall that cites the names of 68,000 downed by war. The longest story their silence can tell is KIA. The parents of these sons have their own damaged hearts from their loss and ours—reminded by the long-lasting marble wall. Some of these parents will never know peace; although today, peace delicately exists in trade. Is greed worth human lives?

There are questions I will never be able to answer—disturbing questions. Maybe explaining how questions can be answered is the part that I play in this writing. There is no class of person who gets answers, but only the choice that one participates in to seek the answers.

Our choices in life are endless, and there are only a couple of choices that change our destiny of moment-by-moment living, day-by-day decisions, or even forever. The choices we make are the only avenues to real freedom, and because we are unique, our answers are tailor-made.

By the choices I made, I am here to tell about avoiding my own destruction. In these cases, I made the right choices, and I am grateful. One of the roads of answers came through a chaplain's prayer while I was in Basic Training—from a dear black man, with eyes of compassion.

Have you ever dealt with the impossible? Have you ever come to the end of your rope? Do you ever wonder what's around the next bend in the road? Have you ever felt completely helpless, with no way out? Have you ever been out on the end of a limb as the branch is being sawed? Have you been so scared you've yearned for a safe retreat? What are the answers—escape, fortune, fame, rank, position?

Join me in the incredible, humorous, unbelievable trip of reality where norm becomes the adventurous and challenging.

The picture painted here is in black and white, but in reality, it's in living color.

Chapter One

Slipping Through the Cracks

L ook at the person on your right; now, look at the person on your left. One of them will be gone from this University of Southern California by next semester." These were the greetings spoken by the dean to all the new freshmen sitting in Hancock Auditorium. The dean was letting us know that we needed to achieve a high standard of academic excellence to assure remaining on the freshmen class roll chart. In other words, it was survival of the fittest.

These chilling words of warning unsettled the audience. In silence and fear, I quietly asked God why He sent me here. I left the auditorium with some fear and uncertainty as well as the underlying feeling of trust after those prayers.

Deciding to give it my best, I found out soon that my best was severely inadequate. My basic problem was reading skills. I read very slowly. What I did read, I had difficulty comprehending. What I comprehended, I had difficulty retaining. These lacks in reading abilities left me almost helpless when it came to performing at the university level. I was an artist, absorbed in my work. I had been so since I first scribbled with crayons as I sat on my Toronto, Canada living room floor. I drew everything and loved it.

My A-B-Cs from As to Bs

Quitting when obstacles face me and things look bad is a dare I'll take any time. My non-quitting attitude started early in life. At five, when everyone in my kindergarten class skipped around the room in a circle, I skipped a few minutes until the one directly in front and behind me fell down. My out-of-step feet caught theirs. The moment of truth became real when the teacher demanded I step aside to view the class skipping without me. I said to myself, *Self, don't give up; you can do it,* and I did after two days of intense practice in my dirt driveway. I found out it's all in the rhythm. Boy, then did I skip, right from there to my bedroom, where I finally slept in peace.

From then on, skipping was my thing. I skipped all the way to Peabody Elementary School in Santa Barbara from my house every day, a little over a mile from home. Then, I skipped around the classroom. As the teacher and other kids watched me, I showed them what skipping was all about.

My skipping didn't stop there, nor did the negatives. Soon, all the other five year olds skipped forward to the next grade as I skipped to a special class for the inadequate.

My mother and counselor both told me I was smart after shoving wood dowels into round holes to see if I could make the right ones fit. When I did the right thing, the counselor called my mother aside and explained, "His problem is not in his brain, it is in his size. He's too tiny for first grade." (I knew I could learn, but growing I wondered about.) Well, I didn't grow, but my learning did in one area, but not in all the others.

I learned to draw; and draw I did. My teachers thought I was another Michaelangelo, and put my pictures all over the school. My ego went wild, but was kept at bay by concern, while teachers warned by mother that I wouldn't ever make it if I didn't learn my ABCs.

When I was five, I drew my first combat art of pirates fighting on ships, like seeing an Errol Flynn movie at the Granada Theater on State Street in Santa Barbara. I also drew portraits of people whom I admired, one specifically being Abe Lincoln, which I proudly hung next to George Washington, painted by my 11-year-old competitor, Dennis Boucher.

My high school achieving efforts allowed me to muddle through basic reading; but that was high school. Now, I was required to perform at university level, where I would discover the necessity to advance beyond the only book I ever completely read (*The Adventures of Huckleberry Finn*). In other words, I was soon to find out that USC was a reading school and my kind was in real trouble.

After receiving an F in dumbbell English, and then a D on my second try, my real problems began when I entered Literature 1. The first couple of days of class were okay; then serious troubles began, as the professor took us on a journey to Henry David Thoreau's *Walden Pond*. When he became lost in the wonder of the pond, I took my own journey into my own little art world of creative expression.

Walden Pond was not truly that boring, but, in comparison to the beautiful ponds and trees I drew through Thoreau's description, I was an artist absorbed in my work. This was my nature ever since picking up a crayon.

The professor must have thought I was deeply into what he was saying, since I feverishly gave my notebook a workout. I'm glad that he never checked to find it was actually a sketch pad. Soon afterward, test day revealed the truth—that I'd never been to *Walden Pond* at all. I bombed out so severely on the test that the professor felt it necessary that we have a little conference. I remember nervously entering his office and waiting for his comments. I found his words short and to the point, however. He waited until I was seated and ready for confrontation. Then, staring at me with intensity, he simply asked, "Why are you here?"

After a lengthy pause, allowing for necessary reflection, he tilted his glasses. As he did this, he gave me a little suspicious smirk as if to say, "Why bother? And who let you in here anyway?" I timidly responded to his put-down comment with an explanation. I told him that I was an artist, hoping that such a comment would give explanation as to my failed performance. In courses, as in life, I see everything through the eyes of an artist. While others were in their literal, I was steeped into the color, shapes, forms, and dimensions. Would he understand? He didn't. Later, however, I found that the put-down comments actually had some mixed-in, hidden compassion. Although he never verbalized compassion, I sensed his feeling through studying his eyes of compassion.

Grade time arrived. I was given a mercy D. The low, but passing grade, combined with the overall negativity of the ordeal, left me with mixed emotions. I felt like a failure, a mental misfit, and asked God why He had made me less than normal. I never heard an audible reply to my complaint, but felt a deep down comforting assurance that everything was okay, in spite of this negative picture.

Walking in the halls of Hancock Auditorium, and through the USC campus by the library, I was thinking about my weaknesses and strengths while capturing the words of Michaelangelo, "The greatest work of art is but a shadow of the divine." After reading this, I thought, *Yes, all gifts come from God, and if God wants me to become adequate, then He will give me the ability. If He doesn't, then He has something else for me to do.* Even though I was comforted by these thoughts, I decided to pursue whatever God put before me. Yet, I still needed a God kind of pat on the back after the English Literature professor incident.

Somehow, I knew that God was in charge of me and actually created me uniquely odd to fulfill some special purpose. Even with this awareness, my pride was crushed and I was hazily confused as to my belonging. My crushed ego needed to get a positive boost.

The desires of my heart became fulfilled as I entered the first in a series of "ups" after that "down" experience. It happened in a way I never could have dreamed or imagined. It happened like this . . .

Chapter Two

A Little Fun at Grade Time

I could hardly wait to see the results. Grades were out and I was headed to my mailbox at Marks Hall dorm. A crowd was jammed at the boxes. We hurriedly grabbed our envelopes and quickly began opening them, tightly crowding ourselves in the elevators.

Everyone was glued to their own grade sheet until they either cried or shouted. I shouted inside when I saw my grade sheet, because a clerical error had done me a big favor. The sheet showed 30 units of As and Bs for one semester. (By the way, that was impossible, since the maximum load for one semester was 18 units.)

It just so happened that there was a business student named Edward Joseph Bowen, III, and I was Edward John Bowen. Yes, I had his grades *and* mine. The other Edward wasn't stupid. He had all As and Bs in about 15 units of business courses. I had all As and Bs in about 15 units of easy art classes (except for my D in English Literature.) The overall picture of 30 units of As and Bs presented an excellent picture.

Suddenly I thought, *Now is my chance to save my crushed ego.* So I did. I conveniently commented out loud in the elevator for all to hear, "This was the toughest semester I've ever been through, but I made it." A few of the guys, now bored with their own grades, started peering at mine, and guess who looked at mine first? It was the Marks Hall genius chemistry major! His ever widening eyes peered through his thick glasses and he gasped while pouring over my grade sheet. Looking bewildered, in disbelief, and with a mouth hanging open he said, "How did you do it? How? Why a 30-unit load is impossible!"

By then, the whole crowd in the elevator was in on the action. With a put-on serious look, I calmly and humbly said, "It's been a tough one. Yes, this semester has been a real challenge for me. I need to get through USC. In two years, so I've gone to the dean and he has given me special permission to take on an extra load. The whole thing has been an ordeal for me and really taxed my brain, but I've done it! Yes, it was tough, but I did it."

You can imagine the talks and stares. I felt so good. I didn't even feel bad about lying, for the good purpose of saving my crushed ego. I argued with myself and, in conclusion agreed that, in this case, it was okay to lie. Then I thought, *Well, maybe it's not; but the all important thing is that I feel good about it.*

What a self-esteem booster event! Things got better for me thereafter. I was riding high. The word seemed to get around; often I would imagine seeing small crowds pointing me out as I pride fully walked the campus. There were hushes and stares and talk about boy genius, a role I always had longed to fulfill. I didn't forget to thank the Lord for humorously rescuing me from my previous "pride crash" and putting me in such good light with my peers.

The crowning event! Graduation from college arrived after some accomplishment. Deemed worthy of participating in this event, we entered the day of ceremony and speeches, feeling very good about ourselves. Being one of them, I felt more than good about myself because I knew my victory was in the realm of miracles. I remember the graduation, festivities, and triumphant music. The final inspirational speech was given by Mark Hatfield. Everyone looked so uplifted and exhilarated as he spoke his inspiring words.

I put on a copied, assured look of understanding and joined in the exhilaration. Beneath the look, however, the real me was in another world. I kept the positive put-on look until I spotted my Japanese genius roommate from freshman days approaching me. With victory cap and gown on, he wore his typical suspicious, sarcastic grin. I was certain I was in for trouble because he knew the real truth about me and often, in fun, used to rub in the negative stuff. Now, in high performance, he congratulated me. Earl never gave me a positive without a negative counter following the positive. He greeted me, "Congratulations, Edward; you are a first!" I responded cautiously with, "What do you mean, Earl?" He jokingly added, "You are the first student ever to graduate from this university as an illiterate." So, I laughed with him. Earl called me Edward (with a tone of sarcasm).

"I'll say a little prayer for you . . ." Earl knew I had faith in God and, deep down inside, he wanted to have this faith for himself, but could never quite reach that point of taking the necessary steps to faith. Very intelligent, Earl seemed entrenched in the negative thinking of the agnostics. I prayed much for Earl and almost gave up, but I knew that there was still hope for him because of his childhood friend in Hilo, Hawaii, Ken—a strong believer in Christ. Ken assured me that he would never stop praying for Earl.

Earl and I were roommates. I don't believe he liked Mainland America as much as his native Hilo. He was a fun guy and joked around like few I have known since. He made life interesting as a freshman, and with our other roommate, Raphael Edgebrook Tisdale II, teased me almost to the breaking point about my weaknesses. I have always had fond memories of them both. Recently, I was informed that Earl passed away from complications from an illness.

Sure enough, USC discovered the mix-up, but it wasn't until I took the bull by the horns and pointed it out to them with the real facts. The clerk laughed and confirmed there were two Edward J. Bowens, I had received his grades, and the records were to be changed immediately.

Chapter Three

The Teacher—
Mr. Bowen

lliterate graduate . . . ," words that lingered and played over and over in my mind. I then decided to defy their application to me and boldly pursue the teaching profession.

During my interview, I could see the look of question as to my appearance being too young. However, after I provided God-given answers from prayer, the interviewer was convinced my mental maturity contradicted my youthful appearance, Acceptance came soon.

I launched into student teaching at my first opportunity at Rosemead High School. What a privilege to work with such an astute mentor, J. V. Montelongo. He was an artist with favor to me, and he gave me the necessary encouragement to carry on.

The student teaching year was somewhat successful. I then landed my first full-time teaching assignment at Villa Park High School in the small town of Orange, adjacent to Disneyland. I'll never forget my first day of teaching. It went something like this . . .

My voice shaking, I began class by saying, "Hi, my name is Mr. Bowen. I'm glad to be your new teacher and am looking forward to instructing you in art this year." These introductory words were etched in my memory. At 6'2" tall and 150 pounds, I shook in fear while facing about 30 high school students. What a moment as a full-fledged, first-time teacher—no more student teacher with a back-up coach to keep me from falling apart. Looking more like a high schooler, myself, my confidence factor was hard to find. Fear soon faded as sympathetic students coached me into confidence, giving me some well-needed security. Eventually, I settled in, assuming that I was in the first stages of a lifelong career.

My art classes were filled with all types. I had the jocks with the lettermen jackets, the cheerleaders with their cute outfits, cute figures, and cute faces. I had the hippies with their little more than long hair (as much as the dress code would allow). I had the rejected, right along with the rest and, of course, I had the gorgeous, one-of-a-kind beauty queens. One particular queen still stands out in my mind, today. She sat in the front row, staring me in the face as I uttered my very first teaching words. At first, her face had a look of wonderment on it as she, along with 30 others, tried to figure out if I was a joke, maybe a younger brother's friend who was filling in for the new teacher. After a while, though, she knew the truth and turned her look of wonder to an unforgettable smile. From then on, no matter what I acted like, harsh or stern, she never took away that smile. I must say, it helped to take away my seriousness.

Another girl I remember well was Sharon. She worked at the local fast-food place and used to load me up with extra fries on my frequent visits. Yet another in the classroom was the class clown who loved attention of any kind. One day another student accidentally knocked over a large bottle of paint onto his head as he bent over. Slowly arising, all anyone could see was Elmer Fudd-looking eyes and nose appearing through all the blue paint, with a sheepish smile. The students roared, and he made his departure very slowly.

Without warning, something happened that radically changed my permanent plans. An official government letter was delivered to me stating, "We have received information that leads us to believe that you are not registered for the draft. Please respond by immediately reporting to your local draft board in order to give explanation."

That trembling feeling emerged once again. I was caught doing the unthinkable; I had never registered for the draft when I was 18 and failed to do so for several justified reasons. First, when I was 18, in 1961, there was no Vietnam War. Second, I was ignorant of the laws concerning draft requirements. Third, when I found out about the laws and requirements, I was in college and assumed that I was deferred from the draft. Further, I was a Canadian Citizen and assumed that foreigners were exempt from fighting in such wars.

Ignorance of the law was no excuse. My assumptions and reasons were, as a lady nicknamed The Cold One put it, "way out of line." But, before elaborating on my encounter with The Cold One, let me tell you what happened next . . .

What would happen? Nervously, I took the letter to the principal, and handed it to him. He took one look at it and, with a perplexed, but confident, look in his eyes, marched to his desk, picked up the phone, and was almost immediately in touch with someone at the State Capitol in Sacramento. After speaking with the state government official, he turned to me in confident assurance and told me all was well. He said, "You need not worry about all this. It's merely a formality and there should be no problem." Soon deferment paper work would arrive for submitting to my local school board to approve. Confidently, I left the principal's office assured that all was well. Shortly I was to find, however, that all was not well.

Entering my local draft board office with the correct papers to sign, I was met by a dark-haired, malevolent lady known, in Riverside, as The Cold One—a name suiting her well. Abruptly she informed me that I was not off the hook and that the local board would review my case. Feeling her glares, I anticipated the board's decision-making letter.

My heart pounded when the letter did arrive and I opened it quickly, looking for the bottom line. This bottom line was easy to spot because it was the only line. I was ordered to report for duty in the U.S. Army on November 28, 1967 and given only ten days to make the decision.

I felt like pretending a decision wasn't facing me; I wanted to ignore the letter and resume life as usual. However, these officially dated orders shocked me into stark reality. One decision would be to avoid orders and take a legal trip to Canada to escape the draft altogether.

As I saw it, America's purpose in this war seemed clouded. Although USC. wasn't a protesting school like Berkeley or San Francisco State, it did have its share of protesters. I remember hearing students screaming four-letter expressions of hate to our government. Hounding voices said different things, which compounded the confusion and made it hard for me to take a firm position. Most of those voices from my peers were those of protest.

The last four years of college, I watched the no-win war on television from my dorm. It was a protest era, involving people like Jerry Rubin. This anti-establishment rebel and protest spokesman was telling his peers to kill their parents. In my memory, it was a time when a frustrated President Lyndon Johnson pushed the unwilling troops on and on for years, hoping for some kind of true victory that would justify a save-face pullout. These times expected men of all views to report for duty and obediently serve their country. I was quite upset.

Like others, I was upset to be required to give my all for something so undefined and so seemingly hopeless. With all this in mind, I must choose now, as The Cold One put it. She said, "You are a Canadian citizen and, of course, you can go back to your country and not fight in this war." But she warned me, with assurance, that if I did so, I'd never be allowed to return to America. She appeared to enjoy telling me this. Her cold glare of authority seemed to represent the force of a determined establishment. Contemplating my options, I left her presence.

Chapter Four

The Before and After Colonel Decision

I confided in my girlfriend Ginger's dad (an Air Force Colonel). Colonel Norris' demeanor resembled that of Chuck Norris. Although he liked me, he did question my worthiness for his daughter. All *those* hopes were dashed after what followed.

Let me paint a picture for you. Imagine today's Chuck Norris as this colonel, just returning from Vietnam after leading his troops in battle. Now, see him at the Thanksgiving table with a skinny 24-year-old pacifist at the other end of the table—one hand under the table, holding his daughter's hand, the other hand shaking while holding a fork with a scrap of turkey hanging from it. Now, picture me saying, "Ya know Colonel, I'm not the military type and I'm thinking about Canada as a temporary home and Ginger accompanying me; what do you think?"

The scene didn't include Patton, but it might as well have. Colonel Norris' retort produced a pat on the back, in the process of escorting me out of the room. After dinner, he addressed me in an authoritative voice, "Ya know, son, the army will be good for you. It will make a man out of you." These were the words that ultimately led me to my final decision.

I decided to be a man and go to Canada, but before I did, I went to my parent's pastor for words of comfort. To my surprise, I found out he wasn't a pacifist at all, and his temper rose when I expressed my feelings to him. He responded just as the colonel had.

I continued to ignore counseling until I found a pacifist pastor who agreed with me. He told me, "The meek will inherit the earth." I knew I was doing the right thing, then, so I left praying a prayer of thankfulness that my meekness was going to keep me out of this war. However, as I prayed, I felt no peace. Peace was the determinant umpire in this threatening war within me. So, I would continue praying until I felt peace.

From there, I asked my parents, friends, and even students what they thought I should do. I reasoned that I could make a quick, legal exit to Canada, which would be great. At the last minute, I even thought of tossing a coin and living with the flip. This really took too much guts, though.

My life and reading were strangers until I grabbed all I could read on the subject, including, incidentally, a book by J. Vernon McGee (whose church I used to go to in Los Angeles during my year at USC) called, *Should a Christian Go to War?* This book swayed me to GO. My final decision popped out of my mouth with, "I'm going! Yes, I'm going to go, and if I die, I die; if I live, I live." Finally, there was peace.

I looked at my buddies who found their escape through physical ailments, school deferments, etc., wondering about their worthiness of escaping this terrible fate. Why was I picked out for a radically altered life that could very easily lead me to my life's end?

Yes, after all options, I chose to follow orders directing me to report for duty. I decided to submit myself to 24 months of required duty. The reality was, shortly I would leave a safe, secure life and go fight in a war that I wasn't even sure I could give my wholehearted support.

With these concerns in mind and determined to commit myself to an unknown fate, I made every attempt to calm down and complete the next ten days with my students.

I announced the news to my students, and saw faces and heard noises of disbelief and shock. Many of them felt it was a bad dream. Anger and sorrow were reflected in their young voices. When the reality finally sank in, they were aware that we had only a few more days together. So they decided to make my last days and times with them so full of fun that I would never forget them. Each day, we had a class party; even the teachers showed. My news spread fast and these precious days were filled with cookies, cakes, and other treats.

The students did make a big fuss concerning my plight, mixing their talk with that of the record player spinning the favorites of the day. One favorite was a war protest song by Peter, Paul, and Mary, highlighting the poor-me thing when, all of a sudden, one of the cheerleaders ran over, unannounced, and pulled the record off as it had begun playing ". . . gone to graveyards, everyone . . ." and shouted, "Enough of the 'poor-me' Bowen stuff. He's going to be OK!" That was it, then, for Peter, Paul, and Mary. Soon, we heard " . . . let's go surfing, now, everybody's learning how; come on, Safari with me."

Then, the final day of school arrived; some students draped banners on my car in the parking lot. The singing and shouting became a very emotional time for me. In only three short months, I had grown fond of these students. Now, leaving them so suddenly was quite difficult. To this day, 30 years later, I still remember their faces as I said my last good-byes in the parking lot.

Considering the prospects of a completely different lifestyle, I was concerned that certain of my unusual hidden traits might be discovered. If they surfaced during the pressures of controlled military life, I knew they would be spotted, and could result in forcing serious negative consequences. How would my creative side deal with required military constraints of all aspects—an unknown fate?

Killed in Action (KIA) often showed up stamped on final exit military papers of two-year draftees sent into infantry or artillery. The years from 1967 to 1969 in Vietnam were exceptionally bad years. Some of the most intense fighting occurred then. As a draftee, there were no choices in determining my course or fate in the war. On the other hand, enlistees who signed up for three or four years could be guaranteed a safe, cush assignment for their tour of duty. These assignments included cooks, mechanics, clerks, language specialists, etc.

Taking these facts into consideration, I thought, *Lord are you really in charge of my life, or am I just a chance being with my fate, marching forward on a purposeless course?* I chose to believe that I wasn't a chance being but, instead, I was one designed by God with a life of planned purpose, even if it was filled with negatives while in route.

Chapter Five

The Morning Mourn

This morning was unforgettable! A dark, drizzly, foggy morning at the Riverside draft board parking lot set the scene.

Before boarding the bus, I thought about the sacrifices my dad and mother had made to send me to college. I remembered how my dad had refused vacations so that he could earn more money, making it possible for me to attend college. I was thinking about the stories he told me about his rough childhood.

Then, I focused on the time when my mother was so proud of my father because he had just won a national speakers award for the best story told—a story of his rough childhood. Yes, I remembered it well. Dad lost his own father in a tragic death, just prior to the Great Depression. With little, or almost no money, his mother was forced to raise six children. At 13, and the second oldest, he had to quit school and go to work to help make ends meet. The rest of the story revealed a life of struggle.

Deeper into thought, I felt how unfair it was for my father to see his only son accomplish something of significance, then watch him being taken away to fight in a war. I wanted to run from what was before me, but I knew I couldn't. Now I was to face whatever was dished out.

This was a morning when fearful, teary-eyed parents said good-bye to their young boys as they boarded the bus and headed for Fort Ord, California.

All types of individuals showed: long-haired, short, tall, tough, smart, and even geniuses boarded the bus. What a surprise! Entering the bus, I rubbed shoulders with a character from my old high school days. What a shock to see him in this crowd, assuming his kind would surely escape the draft. He was well-known not only to the students but to the teachers and administrators as well. They considered him way beyond genius level, beyond the intelligence of an Einstein. I thought, *Looks like the military needs all kinds to join the forces.*

Entering the bus, my shaken 5'4" mother stood next to my 6'3" dad as he encouragingly said, "Son, take care of yourself." I paused for a second, with no response. He said again, "Remember, you are the only one who can take care of yourself." Again, I didn't respond but translated it as, "This is the time to trust in the Lord." Although those words were absent, I knew that was his real intention.

The bus driver didn't give us much time for emotional good-byes. As he drove out of the parking lot, everyone on the bus waved long good-byes to the sad crowd lingering in the lot. The long bus trip to Fort Ord began; soon everyone was loosening up and getting to know each other.

One guy stood out. He was the meek, weak type, and his teary-eyed mom was exceptionally jolted as we left on our journey. Getting under way, the little guy stood up and opened his long rain coat to reveal several bottles of alcohol secured in the lining of his coat. With a smile and bold look of put-on manhood, he passed the alcohol to all the needy men on board. I just quietly watched it all, wondering what would happen to these guys in the next few months and years.

While in route to Fort Ord, we picked up other guys, including one unusual, short, stocky guy named Ron, who sat next to me. He was very confident and began telling me that his future in the military was to be a short one, as he was certain his previous schooling had prepared him for the clergy occupation, ensuring a quick release from military duty. He said his kind was vitally needed in civilian life. As he continued I thought, *I should have been in that bunch, too; but now it was too late for such a deal.*

The best I can remember, this clergyman offered, "You may be going to go through basic training at Fort Ord. You may learn to kill and fight in Vietnam, but I'm not going to do that. Nope, I'm going to see a clerk at Fort Ord, and show him my clergy intent. He will stamp papers with some nice words and then I'm checking out so that I can get on this same bus and head back to where I belong—as a pastor trainee."

Needless to say, I was stunned by his confidence and determined expression. I will never forget it. Even 20 some years later, amazingly, I spotted this same confident face as he hosted Vietnam veterans for Christ at a local San Diego church that he pastored. The vets displayed their wounds, missing legs, and all, and then we all cheered them, including Pastor Ron, as war heroes.

We passed Disneyland on our long 20-hour route to Fort Ord. Fond memories flashed through my mind, even memories going back before Disneyland was Disneyland. I remembered my cousin's dad, Ken, displaying blueprints of a theme park on his dining room table that his acquaintance, Walt Disney, was planning. Ken said that Walt was wondering if he could get an $8,000,000 loan approved to begin the theme park. My dad smirked while Ken continued, "Don't laugh, the kids will love it." Then adding, "Maybe you ought to buy the orange groves right here, as he pointed them out on the map." This, coincidentally, is the exact site of Disneyland today. Well, my dad didn't listen. He figured that we had enough oranges on our own trees in Riverside, so he ignored the suggestion.

To the day of my 12th birthday, July 16, 1955, Disneyland had its grand opening. This day, however, I was watching television of Ronald Reagan cutting the ribbon at Disneyland for the opening while blowing out candles on my birthday cake. Funny, how these things flash back in your mind.

The next week, I had the opportunity to see where those orange trees used to grow. It was hot that day, the crowds bugged me, and I remember watching the clowns grab garbage being tossed before it hit the ground. The park *was* fun, and there was much to investigate.

As I thought of Disneyland, its fun, and the date Disneyland opened, it reminded me of war—and no fun. Exactly 10 years earlier, I had blown out just two candles the same time of the first atomic bomb explosion (July 16, 1945). Then, I pondered the century I was living in, one filled with wars, all seeming so senseless to me. I focused on how terrible Hiroshima and Nagasaki must have been when the bomb rendered the land barren.

Now, at 24, I was leaving the memories behind and heading into a most uncertain future. During the long ride, I chose not to socialize, but rather take the time to reflect and meditate on past experiences. I thought about my childhood difficulties with learning blocks, which caused me, my mother, teachers, and concerned counselors all kinds of frustrations.

I recounted the drag-along trips to counselors with my persistent mother demanding that her intelligent son be taken out of the slow learner classes. I remembered the reluctant counselors and teachers finally giving in to my PTA President-mom's demands. Also, I reflected on how matters were made worse because of my physical appearance. My first driver's license revealed the facts: "Edward John Bowen, Age: 16, Height: 5'5", Weight: 105 pounds." I liked my brown hair and blue eyes, but not my height and weight. Then, I thought about overcoming my physical weakness by joining the high school swim team that forced my weak body to advance.

I wanted to prove to myself that I could be great. Recognition, importance, and the rest were prominent in my mind. It was necessary for social survival. The thought of being somebody in something became intoxicating. "The hard work would be worth it," I reasoned. But it never did work, except to give me pneumonia from overwork, which began my lung problems that have never stopped. Finally, I recalled giving the learning thing my best shot and managing to achieve acceptable grades for entering the university to face challenges that seemed beyond my capability. What a legacy of twists and turns!

By the time we reached Fort Ord, most of the guys were like old buddies. We approached one of the large entrances to the Fort at about two o'clock that morning, while the entrance gate and

Military Police guard stand were almost fogged over. I glimpsed at the MP waving us in and looked at his statue-like, obedient expression in face and stance, I wondered if the heavy, hopeless spirit of this place had overtaken him. Passing through the fog, the gates slowly closed behind us and we were locked in. The whole scene reminded me of the World War II black and white films of Auschwitz or Buchenwald prison camps, with their high fences and cold, empty-looking buildings.

When the bus came to a stop, we were escorted off and herded like cattle into a large, well-lit auditorium where we joined 200 or more individuals who were silently sitting and staring at the empty podium and platform. There, we sat patiently in silence, waiting for the unknown—a wait that seemed like an eternity. I tried to hide and be as inconspicuous as possible. I even made sure that I had a seat very close to the back of the auditorium, next to the exit, even though escaping was out of the question.

Those first few moments in a new military world were unforgettable. Everyone was now in serious thought. We all were tired, cold, and nervous, yet alert. I was thinking a rather strange thought at this time, however, and distinctly remember what it was. "Soon, someone will come to the front podium and will say something, and it will be just one word. It will be an important word, but what will that word be?" This thought kept repeating itself over and over in my mind, nagging me. At that time, it was hard for me to know why such a thought would be so impetuous, except to remember how those significant thoughts cropped up before in my life at crucial times, now and then.

One specific time was at the age of six. My mom asked me to go the store with my sister and buy a lemon meringue pie. Going a step further, she gave me a dollar and an order accompanying it, "Don't spend this money on something else and, whatever you do, don't drop the pie." I obeyed, and all the way down Los Pinos Avenue I kept saying, "I will not drop the pie; I will not drop the pie." Then, I head another voice saying, "You will drop the pie." Guess what happened. You're right. I didn't take a bite, but the pie "bit the dust"—meringue and all, upside down. I tried to resurrect it from the dust, but . . . All the way home I was crying, anticipating the wrath just ahead.

After, I learned about the nagging voice. The voice haunted me, now, until the moment arrived when someone actually did step up to the podium. He was a Second Lieutenant of obvious importance.

Seeing the deliberate posture of authority, everyone seemed to become even more tense. The moment came when that all- important first word was spoken, the first word of authority I would hear as a military man. Before speaking, the Lieutenant stared at the crowd of bug-eyed, new recruits and began to move his head back and forth with a controlling expression and suspicion. He scanned the crowd as if he were looking for someone, and then, suddenly, he spoke his first word, "Bowen." Yes, "Bowen" was his first word. He paused and repeated it by saying, "Bowen; where is Bowen?" I was silent for a moment and so stunned that my name was that anticipated first word I was waiting to hear. I quickly pulled myself together and raised my hand, while all stared in stunned silence at me.

When my raised hand was spotted by the Lieutenant, he simply said, "Come up here." With a pounding heart, I quickly rose and headed for the podium. While approaching, a military policeman came toward the same platform.

All eyes were glued on us as the Lieutenant stared me down and spoke his next sentence. Adding no explanation, he said, "Go with him." I paused and quickly thought, "Go with him, the military policeman, but what for? What have I done?" I looked at the military policeman for some kind of body language response that would give me a clue. He didn't appear to be a kind person. Silently, he marched me out into the cold, dark November night. We took a rather lengthy walk in silence. Thinking I probably should be courteous and say something to break the chilling silence, I said, "Nice night, uh?" He didn't respond, so I shut up.

As we continued the march, I caught a glimpse of his controlling appearance. Behind the look I could read his thoughts. They were, "Don't you realize who I am, and who you are, and where you are? This is military time and I'm somebody. Can't you see my black Army helmet and my MP uniform. Don't you know that you are a lowly nobody beneath me?" Quietly thinking this, we marched on until we finally came to a lonely looking barracks.

He opened the door, but didn't enter. I stared in and noticed that it was a kind of storage place. Off in the corner, nestled in cases of stored objects was a nice, inviting bunk. Looking in, the MP gave me a command, "Stay here until we come and get you." I thought, "Stay here for what reason?" He didn't explain and I thought it would be best if I didn't complicate matters by asking why. I obeyed. He shut me in and marched off.

Left alone, I stood there, amazed, and thought, *I wonder what this is all about? I don't have clue but, Lord, thanks for letting me have a good night's rest.* I never knew a promise like that existed, here. I knew the verse in I Peter 5:7 that states such a principle. It reads, "God cares for you." After prayers of thankfulness to the Lord for giving me the little room, I was soon out cold, under several warm, gray-green Army blankets and dreaming of home.

The next morning, I was awakened by a hail storm, the sound of marching troops yelling a tune in unison, "Your right, your left, your right, sound off." I tried clearing off the fogged-up window and saw a smartly uniformed, radically military-looking drill sergeant barking fierce commands directed toward the new recruits. Their individuality in appearance was equalized; each had their heads shaved to full baldness. I realized that I could be one of them if it weren't for the fact that I had escaped their fate for reasons unknown to me. I began to wonder why I was in this room, why I had been singled out, and for what purpose.

Walking and wondering, once again I became anxious, but decided to venture outside my safe, secure barracks. Hunger began to gnaw at me. Cautiously roaming, I realized I was in a transition locale. A mixture of fresh, new incoming arrivals was being processed along with uniformed troops of all ranks.

Finally, I found the mess hall with all ranks in line. I joined them. No one said anything to me as I waited to be served my first Army meal. I ate in silence. Satisfied, I went out on a personal tour of the scenery and discovered a knickknack shop with souvenirs. After buying some humorous military cards, I headed back to my "safe zone" barracks to a familiar norm. No one had shown up to give me orders yet.

During this precious time, I began writing the cards to all my old buddies and university roommates who were still enjoying the free civilian life. I knew they would get a good laugh out of a detailed account of my first military days. I noted that it seemed I had been put aside and forgotten. The outlandish description included my comfortable, isolated quarters and my personal plans to sit tight for days or weeks, or as long as it took for them to remember me. What a kick they would get out of my humorous situation; so I embellished the letter with drawing myself in positions of ease and relaxation.

As I wrote, I recalled seeing a recent *Time Magazine* cover illustrating a military man named Smith and an article that followed. It relayed how Smith, because of his common name, had been mixed up with other Smiths, muddled by bureaucratic confusion, and was told to go home and wait for orders, which he did.

After two years of waiting, he decided to report back and inform the military that his time of service was up and that he needed back pay for this two-year service. A legal battle of this error ensued and ended in a court case for a while. I never found out if he won his case. Considering Smith's situation, I wondered if, perhaps, I might possibly spend the next 24 months living in the little room, eating at the same mess hall, and enjoying a somewhat limited civilian lifestyle. Later, I found that my buddies really got a kick out of the story.

Hoping for a future of possible oversight, my high expectations were soon brought to the basement of dreams by what occurred next. Late that afternoon, after another dinner in the mess hall, I began to feel confident in returning to my safe zone.

Immediately, a frightful sight appeared in front of me. It was the same MP who had taken me to my room the night before. He marched confidently on a straight path, with eyes fixed straight ahead. I thought quickly and decided not to do anything to draw attention like changing course or speeding into a run. My head and eyes bowed to the ground, we grew closer, eyes not meeting, we barely missed each other. Avoiding collision, he took a double take, paused, and stared fully at my face. His facial expressions showed glints of recognizing me; almost passing, he stopped dead in his tracks, turned his head sharply toward me, and placed his hands on his hips with elbows slightly lifted as if being restrained.

His conclusions aroused an angry face and began to snarl. I got blasted when he said, "Where the blank, blank have you been?" He continued on in this abuse while I tried to remain calm. Finished and waiting for my response, I answered, "I've just been waiting for orders."

The look on this MP's face and his tone of voice indicated someone in charge had blown it. As I figured, they had forgotten me. Quickly, I was marched to that same lieutenant who originally said, "Go with him." He was seated, head down, focused on paperwork. Lifting his head, he expressed the same countenance as had the MP. Looking embarrassed, with shock, he changed to the sneer of blame. He scolded me, "You are the real one at fault in this mess." After a few put-down comments, without solicitation, he added, "Well, now things are really messed up. Your designated unit, the one that you are expected to belong to, has already processed in. Now it's too late for you to join them. Do you realize what a paperwork mess I'm in now? And, all because of you."

While he regrouped his thoughts, I just stood there, saying nothing. The lieutenant continued, "I know what I'll do. We'll just squeeze you into another incoming group and you can go through basic training with them." Reasoning through a solution he added, "This could take some time, Bowen, so you'll just have to go back to your room and wait for us to call for you." Off I went, free to relax again, write more letters, read my pocket Bible, have a few more meals while dressed in civilian clothes, and sleep whenever I desired.

As I comfortably settled down, for a long winter's nap, the MP abruptly marched in without a knock. He commanded I come with him to a private office and join two quiet civilian guys sitting before a military official. Finally, I found why I had been separated from the other new recruits. I was an alien, a Canadian citizen, and the other two guys seated with me now were also foreign citizens. One was a Mexican citizen and the other a German. All three of us were being questioned and singled out for special processing.

Chapter Six

Attention, Private!

S pecial processing completed, I was escorted into a room where I joined a group of new recruits, just arrived. I discovered the majority of these guys had signed for the "cush" National Guard assignments. These were weekend jobs (considered a joke by some) with relaxed orders and more breaks than usual assignments. The smaller, remainder of this group were Regular Army, or RA enlistees, those signing for a four-year tour of duty and guaranteed a safe assignment. Besides the National Guard trainees and RA enlistees, there were the draftees—the ones without choices. "No Choices" meant that the choice of service was left up to the Military war planners who assigned frontline war machine duty to the two-year draftees.

As I entered with the other 500 into Basic Training, most of the group ritually spoke of their good deal. Speaking freely in front of me, they assumed I was one of them. When they discovered that I was a U.S. draftee, they were suddenly embarrassed and began to feel sorry for me. They knew my future could very likely end in doom. Contrasted to the present, they knew that after 10 weeks of tough basic training, they would go home to their safe, secure National Guard unit to play weekend stateside Army games for the next six years.

Word of my plight got around during Basic. Most of my peers began treating me respectfully and some, even the drill sergeants, showed me a unique respect. The mixed thinking and talk of my possible demise provoked me into considering the inevitable consequences of my being sent as a fighter in Vietnam.

I reflected on photos of guys with missing limbs, burned bodies, noses and flesh permanently removed from their faces. Missing body parts and destroyed faces made me squirm. The thought of having a face that girls would run from truly scared me. Contemplating that it might actually happen made me wonder if God would permit it. If He did, how would I relate to Him afterwards? Would I turn from Him; would I become hardened? My mother knew a lady who found herself in that situation after accidentally backing her car over her three year old. Would I become hardened like that if a grenade blew my flesh off? Would I be able to be in a wheelchair all my life, without legs?

My sister, Sharron, had a boyfriend for a while who faced a life in a wheelchair after he lost his sense of feeling from a bullet lodging in his neck while in Vietnam. It paralyzed him and left him a quadriplegic for life. Sharron, with her great compassion, tried to make life better for him.

Caring women have been in our family for generations. Sharron falls in the footsteps of our mother, who volunteered in hospitals filled with the disabled. Our Grandmother, Summerbell, fed Toronto bums during the Great Depression. Great Grandmother Summerbell took in post-Civil War blacks as they fled oppression.

One night, as I watched Sharron's boyfriend struggle, I said to myself, *Oh God, don't let this happen to me.* Before Vietnam I saw graphic photos displaying victims of war with burned faces, destroyed limbs, and masses of scarred tissue. I became enveloped with fear. I knew that God allowed such things to happen to all kinds of people, including the ones who trusted in Him. I knew that He allowed experiences of unexplainable horror to occur, yet somehow brought glory to His Name.

I prayed to that God would deliver me from death and destruction. I asked Him to show an undeserved favor to me by letting me see a positive plan unfold for me. With this petition made, I rested in relaxation. I knew my future destiny was now in the hands of the

One who had made me in such an unusual way, the One who planted me in a seemingly terrible predicament.

As Basic Training got under way, I soon understood the shock of all expected comfort completely being stripped away from my life, as did we all. There was little sleep, little food, untreated colds, sore throats, coughs, etc. Then, a record Fort Ord cold of 28 degrees woke us each morning at five. This unpleasantness, combined with homesickness, made matters worse. The icing on the pain cake was made worse when nasty drill sergeants constantly verbally abused us, dropping us for push-ups on a whim or because a buddy failed in a minor detail.

Some of the pain, however, was almost laughable when fellow victims were ordered to do the dying cockroach. Victims were forced into a frozen-like state with arms, legs, and head elevated, their body fixed to the floor. This was a physically difficult maneuver to perform, especially if your stomach muscles were weak or your body was fat. Often and humorously, whole platoons would be seen lying together while uttering groaning and agonizing sounds.

During our basic training ordeal, I remember the threat of another outbreak of spinal meningitis. To prevent further outbreaks, the barracks' windows were always open, the winter cold seeming to penetrate our army blankets. Our short nights of rest were made quite uncomfortable, and we longed for a hot breakfast in a heated dining room. However, before we could enter this short comfort and eating pleasure, we were forced to stand at attention in long lines. This was preceded by a morning three-mile run. Standing in the long line, we could see the sun rise and feel the cold air blow off the Pacific Ocean and go right through our Army jackets, meeting the cold sweat of our shivering bodies.

Then and only then, after a long wait in line, our hope of being surrounded by a warm building became reality. Before entry, however, we were required to be victorious over the horizontal bar apparatus. Our frozen hands had to pull our weary, sick, hungry bodies past 14 bars so we could drop safely on the other side. If we failed to reach the other side, another penalty faced us. Then, we were required to do push-ups (for the fat guys, who could never make it) or run to the end of the line for another long wait and another attempt at the bars. When success was reached, we were to eat the meal in absolute silence.

More humorous incidents came to mind, when silence was broken; one was in the chow line. After the usual long wait, I had a fellow buddy recruit serve me a meal. I looked at the hot meal behind the glass and watched the obedient servers shove the meager portions of food onto a section of the tray. If the main dish was a small portion, you would really feel let down. Moving in silence from the first to the last server, the guy directly in front of me was being served the main stew dish. He looked at his unseemly small portion which contained no meat. Only a tiny potato bobbed in the weak watery gravy. Suddenly, with an embarrassingly loud outburst midst the silence, he yelled, "Hey, there's no meat in my stew." Responding in defense, the server bombastically yelled loudly, "What do you expect, that's Army stew; sometimes you get meat and sometimes ya don't; next please." To save face, the server doubled my portion of stew. Feeling sorry for the guy, I tried to meet up with him and share my larger portion, but somehow he got directed to a table before I could get to him. I saw him two tables over mumbling while eating his tiny meal.

Another incident took place as I sat in the mess hall eating my meager meal. Six guys were at my table, all eating in silence. I saw a half-dollar-size cookie in the dessert section of my tray. We all were disappointed by such a small dessert being served to us. No one dared to complain, but we all showed disgust and almost laughed at the ridiculous small cookies perched on our plates. Relishing every morsel, a guy named Duarte left the table to get a glass of milk. Returning, he noticed his precious cookie had disappeared. His countenance immediately changed while hopelessly staring at the void on his tray. Breaking the mess hall silence he yelled, "Who stole my cookie?" Everyone checked out the situation. Many couldn't control themselves and began laughing at this poor guy's plight. No one, of course, dared to fess up.

Two weeks later, long after Duarte had put the matter to rest, while having a short break, I pulled out a candy bar—acquired at a dear price from the basic training black market. Duarte and this other guy nicked-named, Fidget eyed the prize. Handing the bar to Duarte I said, "Sorry about the cookie. Although small, it tasted good, but I know this will be even better." He laughed, ripped off the wrapper, and broke the bar into thirds for us all to share the prize.

Chapter Seven

My Buddies

These two guys became my buddies in Basic Training. Even though they knew I had been a high school teacher, they kept the secret to themselves, keeping me from the unnecessary harassment. Earlier, in the chow line during processing and basic training, I had been flagged as a teacher. No one of significant rank noticed, though. One of the food servers burst out loudly, "Hey, Mr. Bowen," and pointing laughed, "So they got the teach, too." He laughed so loudly that I joined him in laughing. Only then I realized he was a former student from high school, my most recent student teacher experience. From that point on, I tried to keep the teaching stuff very low-key. I just wanted to be lost in the crowd. I knew if the ranks found out, they would assume I was smart and make me a platoon leader. If that ever happened, I would have extra responsibility placed on me and, inevitably, bungle the thing while being humiliated and left with no escape.

Hiding the facts of my past and keeping a low profile didn't stop the sudden exposure, forced by the usual daily mail call. As the sergeant called out names and handed out mail, he came to a large letter rolled in a tube. The addressee had the required prefix and boldly printed words, "Mr. Bowen." Sarcastically, he said, "You have something; where are you, Mr. Bowen?" The sarge paused, then stepped forward as Mr. Bowen raised his hand, took the letter, and opened it for all to see. Rolling the 5-foot letter onto the grass, a series of about 100 little letters could be seen, handwritten on butcher paper by my former Villa Park High School students. Many of the letters were packed with all kinds of mushy notes, surrounded by hearts and various other artwork.

After some laughter, I quickly rolled up the letter and tried to escape further comments, but it was too late. The truth was out, and I was in trouble. I could no longer hide or blend into the crowd. I was now expected to perform in a different way.

The next letter was not long or packed with love. It was a short Dear John letter from my girlfriend, Ginger. I wasn't the only one to get such a letter. There were so many of them, in fact, that we all kind of joked about it. As letters continued to flow in, we decided to make a Dear John letter collage and place it at the entrance door of our barracks.

As time passed, we, who continued to get sick, longed to escape into a warm, restful sickbed. As we all knew, the hope of such a thing was out of the question. The pleasure of such a fulfilled desire was reserved for only the extremely sick ones with pneumonia, meningitis, or communicable diseases.

My cough continued, however, whatever method I took to get relief. Removing my green shirt and looking in the mirror, I discovered some wonderful little spots. Their unsightly appearance left viewers aghast. I discovered I had the measles. This was thrilling to learn, because it was probably the only minor disease requiring hospital care, a warm bed, good food, and lots of needed rest.

Settling into my new, comfortable quarters, I was quite content knowing I would enjoy myself. Yet, my stay was soon interrupted by something I never expected.

My new roommate introduced himself and laughingly said, "Hope you enjoy your stay here as much as the last guy did." I knew something was up by his comment. This guy began to perform a series of clever tricks on me. He stole my towels, my dessert, my drinks, etc. and laughed on and on in delight at his success. After a couple of days of tricks, I devised a plan to get back at him.

Since I had been coughing all along, my roommate warned me not to cough around the nurses. This would be a sure sign of a needed shot which, when inserted by a long needle in the bottom, was painful. He emphasized the length and gauge of the very long needle. Considering the truth of his statement, I said, "Well, if it is as you say, how will I know if I'm scheduled for such a shot?" Laughing with an evil snicker he said, "I already know you are going to get one of these shots. I know, because you've been red-tagged. Do you see the end of your bed? Can you see the red tag? Do you see it?" Pausing, with his gleeful smile, he waited for my response. Sure enough, there was a red tag at the end of my bed and I knew I was doomed. Knowing my upcoming fate, he relentlessly continued to remind me of it.

I knew I must pay him back—in humor, of course. Around midnight, when he was out cold, I quietly took the red tag off the end of my bed and placed it on his bed. A little while later, a nurse came around, saw the tag and victim, and delivered the prize. Without warning, the nurse suddenly turned the sick one over and, before any resistance was given, drove the needle into his bottom, forcing him to respond with a loud scream.

After being upset at first, he soon laughed and agreed that he deserved such retaliation. My cough continued, however, and I soon found out just what that needle was all about, again bringing on mutual laughter. Relaxation and fun were soon over, and I resumed the difficult routine of basic training. There were more of these roller coaster events, but I need to take you on the other thrilling parts of my ride.

Chapter Eight

Missing Before Action

Basic training experiences allowed me to see some guys crack under pressure. There were two suicide attempts, several failed AWOLs, and one heart attack, leaving the victim in serious condition. The AWOL made a night escape after making his bed to look occupied, even passed the guards undetected. He soon was caught and brought back for humiliating discipline and punishment. I felt sorry for this person when he told me about his plan to escape to his native Tijuana, Mexico. His failure and punishment put fear in all of us. His name is a shadow, now, but his picture is indelibly imprinted on my mind. I remember him doing a lot of low crawling around the barracks after that.

Springing from Basic, one fellow sprinted from the training bleachers, chased by three drill sergeants into the beyond, like a fox hunt. To our knowledge, this one disappeared into the nether regions.

To get gassed or go AWOL, that was the question. Another trainee, while struggling to secure the multi-dangling straps of a gas mask, heard his sergeant yelling, "Get that thing on your head before you choke to death!" The next thing I knew, the trainee appeared to be gasping for breath with the equipment lying idle at his head. Before I could focus, unbelievably, the drill sergeant was groping for orientation, fallen, while the trainee fled to the unknown.

Because of constant excruciating hazing, the underling of our troops was up for grenade toss. While holding the grenade for practice readiness, the underling froze with the grenade in his hand to the last credible second—still frozen. At this point, the bully sergeants took for cover while each second was mesmerizing to onlookers. Finally, the statue liberated the grenade over the wall before we were all blown to smithereens with dog tags identifying the KIA's in the USA.

Another peer explained during foxhole rifle practice, the sergeant was belittling the trainee holding a loaded M-16 rifle and stepping on his hand. The nervous, pressured rookie soldier, while continuing to miss the expected target swung around to meet his preferred target, the sergeant. Next thing anyone knew, the sergeant's arm—with his stripes was gone—at least he kept his head. Trainees need to be *target* shooters. This one really missed his mark—unfortunate, but true. Tragically, he turned on himself and took his own life.

Our 39-year old recycle had a heart attack while sharing a tent with me. His attack and gasping awakened me, so I alerted a lieutenant and prayed for him.

This meek, frail man with a big heart and great singing voice took delight in making basic training a happy place for the hurting. There were many of us. Well familiar with pain from living in the ghetto, this black man sang songs reflecting his feelings. When the lights were out, as well as the drill sergeants, he would sneak out of his bunk onto the cold floor, pacing down the aisle singing "Amazing Grace." We needed what he had to give, especially the two who had just failed in their suicide attempts.

As Basic Training came to a close, the moment that I feared most arrived. We stood obediently in formation as military orders were read out loud. The others were assured of future security as members of the National Guard or as preassigned enlistees; as for me, I was a focal point, indeed. All knew I was not one of the privileged ones. The drill sergeant looked at me and shouted out the order, unemotionally, "Private E-2 Edward Bowen is to be sent to Fort Eustis, Virginia where he will commence training as a 68–D20 helicopter Door Gunner." In silence, I stood as if I'd just heard a jury read off the guilty verdict and pronounced the death sentence on me. With little show of emotion, I glanced at the saddened faces of my good buddies.

Continuing in formation, I considered the possible consequences for such an assignment. I knew the Army didn't train door gunners to stay stateside and was aware of the obvious prepared plans for such individuals. It was well known that this assignment I must take would most likely end in tragedy.

Thirty-eight seconds to live, known in the Army as the most life you can get out of a door gunner in a Vietnam skirmish. If escaping to live later, you became the silent kind. My next door neighbor in Escondido, California, was a silent type. The house next door was silent, except for the children. Months went by without seeing any adult. One night, however, a great commotion alerted me to a heightened argument with yelling, then screaming escalating into grand pleas for mercy to stop the beating. For several nights, the screaming and beating continued. Then, in my yard one day, my hidden neighbor appeared and began spilling the beans. This neighbor broke silence and started to talk, explaining how he had served as a door gunner in Vietnam.

Words cannot describe the atrocities of battle he witnessed. He told me what he did on his last battle day in Vietnam. Ordered by his commanding officer to go on a destroy mission, he knew he would die that very day. He headed into a hidden fortress of enemy fire power thickly surrounding him. Miraculously, through this barrage of fire, he dodged the thick spray of enemy fire. Amazingly, he headed again back into this nest of Vietcong onslaught and gave the fortress all the hell in ammo he could muster in his own barrage—right into the center of their stronghold. Mad, frightened, and baffled, he annihilated the enemy's position. His response was almost insane with revenge. Even with orders to abandon, he gave another vengeful hit as he screeched hateful words at the top of his voice while firing—livid with raging anger.

My neighbor concluded when explaining that he had a timid demeanor as an obedient Catholic child raised in parochial school, where he was taught never to kill. He further described how he never wanted to kill anyone, how he loved people, loved life, and cherished his wife. War had taken its toll on his precious view of life and turned him into an angry man, twisted with the remainder of Vietnam memories, losing present perspective of normal life. The monster in him raged, and the rage burst when least expected.

Later, these thoughts shook me up, and I questioned God's plans—for good to come to those who are His. Before allowing any more negativity to settle in, I prayed and soon felt the same assurance of God's plan to give me a future and a hope that I previously had.

More positive than before, I left formation to assure my buddies that even though things looked bad for me, I knew somehow God would care for me through any type of situation. Though they seemed to agree, I felt they secretly felt otherwise.

A weekend leave after basic training and I left for Ft. Eustis, where I now could begin new training. Almost immediately, the One I was trusting in would reveal His plan for me to escape my inherent doom through a small crack made just for me. I'll name it "the crack to safety."

Chapter Nine

The Great Escape

I joined over 500 guys at Ft. Eustis, Virginia. At dawn, we lined up to face a high-ranking First Sergeant who addressed us with loud, controlling authority. Before speaking, he reviewed the troops dressed formation that stood frozen, obediently in an unspoken hush. Mentally fixed in expectation, we waited for his first words. Getting to the point immediately, he belted, "You privileged ones are all assigned here to be trained as helicopter transmission mechanics and door gunners. The next 10 difficult weeks of training will be intense, at which time you will be trained to be killers. You will also be prepared to die, if required, for your country. When your training is completed, you will receive further orders and most of you will go to Vietnam. Serving there, many of you will die." We all buckled (internally) under the pressure of these stinging words. The sergeant concluded with his final words, "All this said, I want to make one more thing clear. No one has ever gotten out of this training school, and I assure you that no one ever will. In other words, your future is fixed."

Although the sergeant didn't spell it out in exact detail, his implication was of doom for all. I listened to him intently and thought, "I wonder what kind of hatch I'll find to escape this seemingly impossible situation." Considering the possibilities of such an escape, I prayed, feeling an assurance and awareness that such a fantasy would actually become true reality. I was going to get out of this school, "But how?" I thought. Surely no man had the power to get me out of this mess. Only God, Himself, could provide escape from this impossibility. Flooded with confidence, I felt such a great peace about it that I shared it with my stunned buddies. I tried to break the negative shock by injecting humor. The guys thought I was joking when I told them I was going to get out of this school. They responded in ridicule, "Yea, sure Ed. You're getting out and so are we, in body bags sent back from Vietnam."

I persisted and shocked them with, "God will get me out. He has a good plan for all those trusting Him, and I am one of those trusting, expectant ones. I expect Him to help me get out of here." You can imagine how these comments went over. They all thought I was a religious nut. Although serious about my comments, I didn't want to come across as weird, so I attempted to inject a little humor in sharing. My peers heard me reminding them that the only way I was going to Vietnam was as a skinny chaplain who would give them their last rights.

Most of the guys weren't sure about me. But, my roommates were to find I was serious. They learned that my confident boasts and attitude were to be taken seriously. They began to wonder if there might be some truth in what I was saying. On the surface, however, they jested with derogatory words against my strong stand, hiding their true thoughts, cautiously watching the strange and unexplainable events unfolding before their very eyes.

Going to pot, avoiding the dish pit of chatting with shattered dishes, I advanced to the luxury of potato peeling. Two weeks later, we began the Advanced Individual Training School. A plot also began to unfold which would provide the vessel for my great escape.

This school was a combination of door gunner and helicopter transmission training. The word, mechanic, and the learning requirements of this training threw me into silent panic. "Mechanic" was the "M" word, recalling as a boy my resistance to mechanical things.

As a young lad, I was not mechanical. I was talked into building a go-cart with my buddy, Lane Cash. He understood more about mechanics than I, yet somehow convinced me to expand my horizons into the world of mechanics. My life savings of $17.00 became my first investment into the new world of a mechanical project. With only $3.00, Lane wanted to merge his investment to compound $20.00 of financial capital. So, during spring break, Lane's mom's lawnmower became the perfect specimen to launch our mechanical go-cart masterpiece. National Geographic magazines comprised our motor mount. Satisfied with building this wonder, and with full assurance our go-cart was a masterful invention, we found extra parts became essential in keeping this thing alive. Costly parts required advanced capital, and my dad was the closest risk at hand. With raised eyebrow, Dad came through with the loan and the hardware store became our next stop. Our invention zoomed around in the block successfully at least once. Determined to succeed, we ran deeper and deeper into the valley of "debt" for success. Lane "wised-up" to our flop; both cents and sense dwindled. When our go-cart's guts fell out and it ceased to exist, Lane made his exit. My life as a mechanic had passed. Yes, Lane Cash cashed in on the deal.

For the rest of Spring Break, I tried my best to resurrect the go-cart. At giving-up time, Mike Napier came to the rescue. Shrugging his shoulders, but with a willing spirit, he helped me pick up the pile of junk and transport it to my backyard, where my heavy investor could view the heap for more than a year. This go-cart had to go—one way or another. Needless to say, my days of mechanical creativity were gone forever. I chose to concern myself creatively by drawing and painting, instead.

At the beginning of transmission school, I became more interested and preoccupied with my art than I was with the elaborate blackboard charts of helicopter transmissions. Seated alphabetically, I viewed the charts from the front row. I drew pictures and listened, drew more pictures and listened less, and finally drew more pictures and didn't listen at all. I found this to be therapeutic and enjoyable, and it went undetected until test time, two weeks later. The results were not difficult to imagine. I flunked test one. As a result, I was called into a private office for a little heart-to-heart chat. The scene was not reminiscent of the old USC days when my nice English teacher asked, "Why are you here?" Instead, it was "You are here by order of the United States Army, and you'd better shape up and do so quickly!"

This time, I was greeted with preliminary, courteous words that were followed by a quiet, leaning-forth posture. The cautioning bottom line was this, "No one can hear this, Mr. Bowen, but just as a friend, I've seen your records and they reveal that you have had five years of college. I think I know what you are up to." I humbly replied, "What is that, sir?" "Well, we know your kind here," he said. "We have a word picked out for ones like you. It's called, 'shirker.' Yes, and just in case you don't understand the word, I'll do a little explaining by saying you are one of those easy-going learners who likes the recycle routine. You know, you just snail along in order to eat up military duty time, to get set back or be reassigned to a more exciting, non-threatening military occupation such as a cook or clerk."

As he continued on, I just sat patiently, not responding until he made a firm request. Then, I tried to explain that I was preoccupied with my love of art and had never functioned well as a mechanic. With a somewhat you've-got-to-be-kidding-me-look, he gave me some more friendly advice. He said, "If I were you, I'd give this school all you've got. I don't know if you are aware of the fact that this is considered in military circles as a rather elite school; in fact, many enlistees long to come here." I listened intently to his remarks and put on a humbler yes-master face, quietly concealing the real me.

Thinking, *I don't intend to finish this school so I can have the honor of joining the elite ones who are going to Vietnam and will most likely end up in a mass of twisted helicopter parts. Instead, I plan to leave this school and go . . . I don't know where.* Some more encouragement from the Liaison Officer and I was sent out with what he considered a new outlook for me. Actually, I did feel a little inspired after the pep talk. In fact, I even tried to succeed this time and went as far as to put my art pencil down to give it the old USC try.

Guess what, sports fans? The game got worse. Yeah, I flunked the next test. Just like when I was a boy, drawing the complexities of electrical components and their process was a snap and illustrations perfect. Now, 15 years later, drawing the intricacies of helicopter components was exact, yet the whys and the wherefores didn't get through to me. At least I'm consistent.

My failure was not due to the lack of attempting to learn. On paper all was good, but mechanical details were not computed in my brain. Therefore, electrical and mechanical charts became more and more complex as class proceeded. I felt I was on overload, so much so that my brain shorted out.

Things became indelibly worse. Back in the young lieutenant's office, the scolding held no features of a kind warning. Trouble was upon me; and to make things worse, my two finger-pointing buddies now rubbed in the old "good performance, teach" talk. We even laughed over my pitiful test scores. Their laughing and negative stuff prompted me, again, to crave another heaven-sent ego boost. As usual, one was sent, and I did find an escape exit. The scenario was unexpected and unusual.

Each morning, all several hundred of us would line up in the dark. After the usual verbal abuse directed to the tired, cold, and hungry, we would go to breakfast, get back in rank, hear another abusive speech, re-form into marching rank, and go forward in single file. Proceeding forward one half a mile to our usual school room goal, we passed through a beautiful Virginia forest. Something caught my attention, intruding my thoughts, and I became overwhelmed in frustration, replacing my usual calm meditative thinking. The frustration seemed to be set in cement.

Firmly, I decided I could not, or would not go to that class one more time. I prayed, "Lord, please help me; please lead me out of this hopeless mental frustration and exchange it for something enjoyable, fulfilling, less heavy." While praying, I began experiencing an overwhelming feeling of calm, blended with the profound need to be free.

Interrupted, I refocused to action, march, and the ordered words, "Give me a left, right, left, and your right, your left . . ." **and I left**. I left right out of formation and made by own single man march into the beautiful Virginia forest. Yes, I did the unthinkable, I went AWOL (Absent Without Leave). It was a new day for Mr. Bowen. Like old times, I was free and felt so good, at least, at first I did.

Making my quick, almost unnoticed exit, I looked back for a swift glance at my buddies. They were still keeping beat to the marching tune. Immediately I noticed two or three stunned guys who had been marching right behind me, closing rank and continuing on a forward march.

I experienced the beautiful sunlit green forest surrounding me as I wandered, until I came upon a little green meadow with a pretty little stream running through it. All I needed to make the travel package complete was a blanket and pillow. Then I would be ready for rest and recuperation. Since no blanket or pillow existed, I just laid down on the grass for a nap. Settling into comfort, I slept, but was awakened by a couple of deer seeking refreshment and refuge in the same place. They kept me company for a while as I read my new Gideon pocket Bible with the New Testament, Psalms, and Proverbs.

I don't remember what I read, but remember it being comforting and faith-building. It may have been Psalm 139, which says, "I've scheduled every day of your life before you began to breathe." It could have been I Peter 5:7, "God cares for you." Maybe it was the familiar Proverb 3:4-5, "Trust in the Lord with all of your heart and don't rely on your own understanding. In all your ways acknowledge Him and He will direct your paths."

After a quiet time of undisturbed solitude and prayer, my soul became still. Two or three hours later, in stillness, my emotions began to turn. The reality of what I had done began to set in and, apart from a miracle sent from God, I was doomed. I would like to add that I was calm, cool, and full of faith at that time, but that would be a lie.

What next? My soul was somewhat troubled and I began to analyze myself and my emotional makeup. I knew I was not normal and wondered why God had created me with such lack in areas I considered vital in order to make it safely through life. I wasn't angry with God for making me different, but I did question His wisdom in the matter. Deep down inside, however, I knew He had created me a little unusual for purposes that only He understood.

I was confident that what God required of me now was not to get angry, frustrated, and be in a state of hopeless despair. He wanted me to wipe away any tears resulting from a poor-me attitude, get off my comfortable meadow bed, stand up, brush off the dirt, and head out confidently on a single-man march to who knows where. "But, where was 'who knows where'?" I wondered. My Maker needed to affirm me with divine intervention.

Standing at attention, waiting for divine orders, I began to talk to God, straightforwardly. I gave Him all my pent-up feelings of frustration and fears. Even though an audible response was not heard, I just knew He was listening and had already taken action on my behalf. As this assurance lingered, I began to feel a great peace. I began thanking Him for the mess I was in. Doing this, I seemed to feel an even more solid assurance flooding my soul, and I began making prayer requests. As I prayed, I wasn't making specific requests, but I did ask that whatever He chose to do with me would not only be His will, but would also bring glory to His Name. Peace and assurance followed these wrestlings of petitions to God, and I further sought immediate direction from Him.

I walked, prayed, and waited until directive awareness was sparked. The directive came two hours later. It came in the form of a repeated idea pounding in my brain. The thought was simple, "Go to the top; then, go to the highest person in charge. Remember, then, I'm over him; I outrank him." These thoughts rewound, playing over and over. I said to myself, "The highest person in charge could only be the First Sergeant, the one that everyone fears so." I tried dismissing this thought and looked for another, easier approach. There wasn't one. I knew what I must do.

Completely abandoning any good for myself or future, I approached the First Sergeant's Office. You don't just charge into his office. First, you must go through the proper channels and, in this case, it was the front desk clerk. Cautiously, I approached the front desk, and was abruptly asked my need. I said, "I need to see the First Sergeant; we have personal business to discuss." Somewhat baffled, the low-ranking clerk turned, proceeding to march down a long hallway. Returning and still looking baffled he said, "The First Sergeant will see you right now."

Right now! Couldn't I have just a few more minutes to change my mind, maybe? *No*, I thought, *Now is the time for me to make the decisive move.* On I pressed, having tossed feelings of fear, hope, excitement and, finally, total abandonment to the will of God. I neared the door, knocked, and heard a stern, "Come on in." I sheepishly peered through the door and looked to the left—my first look at the famous, feared First Sergeant. His shiny black helmet was off. I could see his strong gut and somewhat boyish facial features. He was a Harrison Ford look-alike.

I was penetrated by piercing green eyes, giving me a good once-over, as he spoke. I heard these same words uttered once before from a figure of authority, "Why are you here?" Coincidentally, I wanted to blurt that I was asking myself the same question over the last three months. Instead, I answered, "First Sergeant, I'm in the wrong school." I stopped there, without further explanation, and waited for his response. Waiting, I noticed the stern expression of authority began to transform before my eyes. Not only did his face change but his pitch in voice raised to the question, "Well, what would you like to do?" It was as if an unseen force was taking control. I heard the voice more like a concerned mom talking to her little hurt boy, rather than the critical tone of a harsh sergeant talking down to his subordinate. The phenomena hit me and I quickly retorted, "First Sergeant, I'm an artist and I like to paint." Suddenly he threw up his arms, rolled back in his chair and said, "Oh, you're just the man I'm looking for." While holding on to my composure, I looped into a state of disbelief. Continuing, he said, "Can you draw and paint?" I said, "Oh, yes! I sure can and would love to do it!"

Shortly, I became involved with giving him the rundown on my experience. I had peaked his interest and it was growing. I explained how I hated helicopter school—I guess I didn't use the word "hate," thinking it might offend him. I went on to explain how I wasn't functioning to the expected standards because my mind was stuck on more serious matters, mainly doing art work.

We both became more excited about art, now. We began talking about illustrating helicopter battle scenes. I described the colors, lighting, mood, and he was talking about the Chinook helicopter. He then challenged, "Can you paint one of these for me?" I responded with, "That shouldn't be a problem! In fact, I think I can do a real good job on such a project." I was immersed in planning the whole thing out in my mind. He was telling me where I could get paints, canvas, etc., and finished with his orders for me to do it. The orders meant, right now! I assured him I could complete the assignment in three days, if uninterrupted. He retorted, "I'll hold you to it."

After an hour of talk, we became like old friends chatting on a first-name basis. He said, "Good-bye, Ed. I'll see ya in three days." I left seeking a refuge for a good belly laugh and quiet time in prayer, thanking the Lord for delivering me once again.

My quiet time of laugh and praise quickly came to a halt as I noticed the troops, led by my platoon sergeant, arriving back from a hard day's work in the shop and school. As they drew nearer, I saw a livid looking platoon sergeant jump out of his marching command position, leaving his troops standing in place, while he came over to personally address me with verbal abuse in front of the platoon. Well . . . I was just waiting for this one. I really needed a little ego boost. While making sure the troops were listening, I answered this barking sarge's question of, "Where the blankety blank have you been?" Calmly I said, "Oh, Sarge, didn't you know? I've been with the First Sergeant today; yeah, we've been on kind of a special assignment together—personal business, you know."

Need I say more? The platoon sergeant froze in complete bewilderment, shocked. I tried to act nonchalant while peering at his blank, distant expression that signaled he was searching for an explanation. I did everything I could to contain myself and keep from guffawing. Somehow, I kept my cool and explained to him about my orders to paint a helicopter battle scene for the First Sergeant. I ensured that my inquisitive buddies were within ears' distance for this news. While explaining, I thanked God for coming through for me.

The platoon sergeant became anxious to be filled in privately about the details of my orders, as he dismissed the troops for a side-line chat.

Pulled aside for the little chat, he asked me what had really happened, and I began filling him in with the details of orders from the First Sergeant. With envy and a puzzled look of awe he said, "Don't you know who the First Sergeant really is?" "No," I said. "Well, he is the most important one ever to be on this post—only here for a while—to fill in for our permanent sergeant. Didn't you notice those golden stripes wiggling all the way down his sleeve?

Well, those stripes tells us that he knows everyone important in the Pentagon, and now he knows you."

Pausing, I began to reflect on what had just been said. The platoon sergeant concluded our short session with a rather vulgar, but descriptive, explanation of what had just happened. He said, "Ed, you are the only one that I've ever known that can step on . . . blank . . . and come out smelling like a rose." Only after many more talks later and private sessions with my inquisitive buddies did I have a good night's rest. The next day, I was off to get my paints, canvas, and sketch pad. Then I went searching for the Chinook helicopters to sketch and capture them on film for reference.

My next venture found me setting up my little art studio next to my bunk. Just beginning preliminary sketches, the corner of my eye caught my not-so-laughing buddies and others watching me put everything I had into a battle scene, a scene that could actually help me get out of true battle.

I put everything I had into this painting. It was good for me to receive some recognition. I asked God to help me make this painting look spectacular. Even though I was never satisfied as an artist, I am certain God helped me finish this one, making it much more than satisfactory.

The timing for working on the painting was perfect because I began the task on a three-day weekend. Most everyone was off duty, heading for fun and escape, and I almost completed the painting without anyone bugging me. I needed a couple of more days to perfect this work since details were still incomplete at the end of the weekend. That turned out to be no problem.

My finished painting illustrated a Chinook helicopter with soldiers exiting it into battle. I was on my way to see the First Sergeant for his critique now. He smiled, paused, and then showed jubilant satisfaction accompanied by many complimentary words. After a little more art talk the sergeant said, "This painting is beautiful. It needs to be hung for everyone to see!" Mulling it over, he decided to hang it in the mess hall.

Now, it just so happened the Colonel was inspecting the mess hall that very day. When he saw my painting, he and the First Sergeant became involved in a head-to-head exchange. Evidently this was a good one. Before I knew it, I was once again back in the First

Sergeant's office discussing more art work. Both the Colonel and the First Sergeant must have agreed for me to proceed with more art, of course requiring a little private spot conducive to artistic inspiration.

Moments later, the First Sergeant suggested, "I know just the place, it's kind of out of the way, located in the forest and close to a meadow. There, you will find a shack that will be perfect for you to create in quiet, undisturbed solitude. First, you must clear out a few old tools. Then it will be ready."

The finalizing arrangements for me to begin work in my new quarters were made and I was given my first assignments. I began by painting artistic signs with words like "Keep Off the Grass," incorporated into clever cartoon designs. From there, I advanced to more artistic creations with detailed Fort logo designs carefully painted on porcelain plates. Creating this artwork was truly easy and a pleasurable task. It was not, however, the ultimate of artistic fulfillment, but the dream deal for a Private with no choice in what was expected of him. It was truly refreshing. Special food provisions, prepared by the head cook who loved the Mess Hall painting, gave me even greater pleasure. The cook went way out every day to prepare some of his favorite specialty dishes for me. What sack lunches these meals made!

All this special attention given me created quite a reaction from my not-so-laughing-anymore buddies. No one else was laughing either. They all were in shock as I lined up with them each morning at 5:00 o'clock, holding my sack lunch in one hand and brushes in the other. They wanted in on the deal, too. A few of the pushier guys sought my help to task them as my assistants in my artistic responsibilities. They wanted to help clean brushes, mix paints, or even clean up after I'd made a mess. How ridiculous; even so, I did manage to pull off the deal a couple of times. Then, we had a ball—sack lunches and all, and I even showed them how to paint. This new routine continued for several weeks.

Well aware that much shirker time was being eaten up all the while, I still had no real direction. Graduation was fast approaching, and soon the qualified ones would receive future orders. *What was to happen to me?* I mulled. My knowledge of helicopter transmissions was a myth and I was totally unqualified to be a helicopter door gunner in Vietnam.

One day, while meditating on my strange set of circumstances, I was called to the First Sergeant's office for another chat. I distinctly remember approaching the front desk where the friendly, smiling First Sergeant warmly greeted me. Getting to the point he said, "Ed, you have done me a lot of favors by doing this wonderful artwork; in return for your job well done, I've done a little behind-the-scenes work on your behalf." My heart pounded with excitement. The words he spoke live in infamy to me. These were words I had longed to hear, words that only could have been inspired, planned, and directed by God! These words were, "I've had your orders changed. You are getting out of this school."

In dead silence, the words repeated themselves in my mind. I was aware they defied those previous terrifying words spoken by the same man who was now addressing me directly. Several weeks earlier, his paralyzing, threatening speech sent piercing chills down the spines of the troops when he barked, "No one has ever gotten out of this school, and no one ever will. Your fate is sealed in cement." Switching gears and refocusing to the present, I was hearing from this very same person who expounded, "I will get you out of this school." What an unbelievable change!

Then, I privately had a session of silent prayer and praise. Even while praying, I heard the sergeant continuing his conversation by apologizing and explaining that he had attempted everything he could do to get me into an art-related military assignment, but he had been unable to accomplish the task. He had, in fact, personally made many efforts to influence the higher ups that I should be doing artwork for the Military. He had even displayed many of my college art slides to key people while on different jaunts to the Pentagon. Further, he even went to the extreme of having me fill out paperwork, hoping I would be accepted as a combat artist in Vietnam. After all efforts were made, he informed me that his attempts were futile and failed to manipulate military orders.

Now, the First Sergeant explained, "You know how the Army is, Ed, with predetermined orders and all; ya just don't change things that easily. But, I've done the next best thing." Intently listening to him, I heard his message like this, "I've had your orders changed, and you will now be trained to be a clerk. You will learn to type, do reports, and various types of office work. It's a wonderful assignment and, to make matters even better, you will get your training in a beautiful fort tucked in the hills outside Tucson, Arizona. As he finished telling me the good news, he smiled with a look of satisfaction that seemed to say, "Look what I've done for you. Aren't you glad?"

I responded with a smile, too, and expressed my grateful thanks. Hidden underneath my smile, however, lay my true feelings of terror because I knew something he didn't know. I knew that not only was I not the mechanical type, but also I was not the clerical type. I knew that if I faced doing paper and clerical work, inevitably I would bungle it up so badly that I would surely come face-to-face with severe consequences.

These thoughts flashed in my mind, but I continued a surface, amiable, sentimental last good-bye to my friend, the First Sergeant. Even though everyone viewed him as a tough guy, I could see a little kind spot in his eyes as he wished me the last good-bye.

Leaving him, I paid my last visits to my buddies who were still stunned and no longer laughing. All of them remained in shock, and I repeated the exact phrase I had spoken to them several weeks earlier during that dark introduction morning. I said, "I'm getting out of this school!" They sought further explanation. I must say that my satisfaction in telling them what getting out was all about was shared with mixed feelings. I had real compassion for these guys, who now had become my good friends. Aware that they faced a future of great risk to their lives, I wanted to tell them more about the God who had rescued me; but time was up for any more talk.

Time to process out within the next hour and be gone, never to see them again. I remember three of the guys by name, to this day. After almost 30 years, remembering their names must be a miracle, since usually I forget even my present good friends' names. I distinctly remember Bob Marks from Seattle, Jim Quillin from Los Angeles, and Tim Carrol from San Jose. I don't know what happened to Bob and Jim, but I believe Tim was killed in Vietnam. My last deed to perform before processing out was to leave a note under Bob Marks' pillow. The note was short and simple, but said a lot to Bob, "I'm gone," and that was it. I was gone.

I needed to go through several offices to process out of helicopter school. Going from desk to desk, I was met with the same usual reaction at first—a casual glance at my forms and then a gasp, followed by a double take. Often I heard something like this, "You can't do this. This is against Army regulations. You are listed as a 68-D20 qualified helicopter transmission mechanic, and you have never even taken the required exams necessary to be approved as qualified."

After the clerk showed the paperwork to a lifer, he came back with an, "Oh well, I guess the Army knows what it's doing." Approved signatures on the forms, I began to get a little nervous. I thought, "What if somehow I end up in Vietnam and am then asked to fix up a messed-up helicopter transmission? Worse yet, what if I'm asked to put the Jesus nut on the helicopter all over Vietnam?" By the way, in case you don't know, that's the name they give to the nut that holds the rotor to the chopper, the nut holding everything together. If it falls, down goes the chopper to certain destruction. The name is surely appropriate. What would have happened to the Vietnam War if I had been working on those choppers. I wasn't, and we lost the war for other reasons.

Chapter Ten

Slipping Through
More Cracks

After helicopter school, I was off to Ft. Huachuca, Arizona, to find what was in store for Private Bowen. The fort was as the sergeant had explained, a beautiful little fort tucked in rugged, high desert mountains outside Tucson. I was in high spirits when I arrived there and had just witnessed God moving miraculously. My hopes and anticipation of great good awaiting me were pushed along by my new, unchallenged faith. My hopes were to be dashed to another low, however.

It was the beginning of a hot summer. I would soon find out that my clerk school didn't begin for several weeks, which meant that the Army had to find something constructive for us to do. In other words, we needed to have our minds, our wills, and our emotions totally consumed with mundane duties during the spare moments between sunrise and sundown. These spare moments were really all-consuming days.

The day, as usual, began at 5:00 A.M., with about 500 of us standing in silent formation and singing a welcome-up tune to the rising sun. After the sun had risen, an angry sergeant barked out orders for the day. Arbitrarily, our chance selection produced our orders and assignments. The tasks varied from choice jobs to dreaded ones. Doing laundry service or picking up lost golf balls on the fort's golf course were among the choice duties. The most dreaded of all duty was KP or Kitchen Patrol.

Our first morning, I was selected for KP. After one day of trying to create artwork out of a dirty dish pit, I was fed up and longed for the next sunrise, when I would surely be selected for the lost-golf-ball duty. As expected, I didn't get my way. After the second, third, and fourth days of KP duty, this negative experience was getting very old, fast. More days of KP, counting right past my 10 fingers, I then began counting on my big toe. Surely, this couldn't keep up; but it did. In fact, I was picked for KP 17 days in a row. The morning of the 18th day, I said to myself, *I've had it; this thing has got to be rigged.* Then, I decided to unrig it and do something very risky but rewarding, if it could be pulled off. I settled on shock treatment for my solution. *If I wait until my name is just about to be barked out by the sarge, I'll quickly jump out of formation, get right up close to the sergeant, and tell him that I'm an artist and I need to paint for him,* I thought. Considering the craziness of such a move, I prayed and asked God to help me with this plan.

Reasoning with God I thought, *Since He is a God of fairness, surely He had seen my plight and could rescue me again as He has in the past.* After prayer and built-up confidence, I decided I must not hesitate, but move quickly and decisively. My heart pounding, I made my crazy move. It happened so fast that no one knew what to think, including the barking sergeant, who was so stunned by the move that he just stood in silence, waiting for me to explain my actions.

Wasting no time in making my next move, I spoke quickly and clearly by saying the identical words I had said during Rescue I, with the previous First Sergeant. I said, "Sergeant, I'm an artist, and I like to paint." I added, "I can and will do a painting for you." As he was still speechless and seemed to be sizing me up for either a kill or a reward, I continued, "I've done art work for the last sergeant I served, and he loved what I had done for him."

Suddenly, the sergeant broke silence and said, "Good, stand over there, and we will talk." As all this was happening, I'm sure the guys still standing in obedience were wondering what this was all about. Soon, they found out as they came back from a hard day's work at KP duty and found me working in my little art studio next to my bunk.

After formation broke, I assured the sergeant my art talent was real. The assurance included explaining that my former experience with the other sergeant was secure and successful. This sergeant began to get excited and said, "Can you paint me some pictures?" I replied, "Sure can, Sergeant. What would you like?" He said, "Come to my barracks and I'll show you." Entering his barracks, he headed straight to his private desk and pulled out some photos of himself taken when he was in Vietnam. He looked at his prized photos admiringly and smiling with a questioned look on his face said, "Can you reproduce these and kind of spice them up with jungle backgrounds and add a little drama by making me look like John Wayne after a battle victory?" He added, "If they come out like I imagine, I could send them to my Mom. She would love that." I assured him that such a task would be no problem for me and I would be glad to take it as a challenge.

The sergeant became even more excited now and said, "What do you need to complete the job?" I answered, "Very little, since I already have paints and even a small canvas board." I explained how I worked best in an environment of peace and quiet. He considered my barracks a good enough place for me to set up shop.

Immediately, I started the project and was well under way with the job when my buddies arrived. Again, as in the past, my envious buddies watched on as I finished the job. After a couple of days or so, I finished the painting, took it to the sergeant, and he was truly pleased. He said, "Mom will love this. Thanks, Ed." Then, he gave me sad news. He told me that he was being transferred to another unit. So, before I could continue on as an artist, I had to close up shop and go back to KP duty. But KP duty wasn't an everyday thing from then on. The curse was broken. Now I had the privilege of working in the laundry room and pulling off clean bedding from a conveyer belt apparatus from sun up to sun down. By the way, I never did get to pick up lost golf balls from the golf course. The Lord knew my weakness, and knew I might wind up being tempted to find a golf club, ending up as part of a foursome platoon.

While waiting for clerk school to start, I continued the menial tasks. Looking back, I enjoyed the fact that I had slipped through yet another crack. I wondered, now, what the future would hold and if there would be more cracks ahead. I didn't know at that time, but the Lord was already going before me, preparing another escape, followed by another one of His glorious victories. The escape crack became more like the Grand Canyon than a slit. Only the Lord could have put this one together.

Events of humble lowliness became heights of glory and victory. These were unfolding experiences sealed with the assurance of truth from Proverbs 3:5-6. Since then, I have memorized the Scripture that goes like this: "Trust in the Lord with all of your heart and don't rely on your own understanding. In all your ways acknowledge Him and He will direct your path."

Chapter Eleven

The Grand Canyon— No Crack

M enial tasks over, we began clerk school. We were all in a state of readiness to give our best efforts for this next challenge. Feeling privileged because we would probably never see Vietnam combat; nevertheless, it was necessary not to flunk this school. Since this school involved simple tasks such as typing, filing, and office work, it shouldn't be a problem.

My confidence was up as I was seated alphabetically in the front row. Once again, I was behind a typewriter and feeling confident that I could do better than I had done in my 8th grade summer school typing class. I remembered that experience being cut short just when I was hitting the 12 words-a-minute mark. My friend, Mike Napier, and I had been kicked out of the class by a ruby red-lipped typing teacher for chewing bubble gum. Mike was a good typist and, in fact, types exceptionally well as a Phoenix, Arizona, attorney.

Typing 12 words-a-minute tops, I still made it through five years of college without typing. That was easy. I'd just pay to get my papers typed. It would run about $5.00 a paper. Since I made good money as a dormitory kitchen hasher (even made as much as $34-a-day as an extra in war movies—imagine that, how ironic), there was no problem. One of the movies was *Von Ryan's Express*, a

Frank Sinatra war movie, and I made $34 a day wearing pink shorts to make me appear nude. I would have made $44 a day, but then they would have had all of me—no way!

Here I was facing the typing challenge once again, and I felt somewhat excited as I quickly caught on. Soon, my mind began churning. I couldn't concentrate. Matters worsened as my buddies, sitting behind me, who were mostly good typists, began to take off and excel. Some were already at 50 words a minute by the end of the first week. My concentrated attempts to master the keys were voided as I sat there hunting and pecking the keys. These guys sounded more like machine gunners than typists. Overall, the noise bothered me. I tried to get control of myself and make some kind of headway, successfully, but all was in vain. My mind just began to cram and refused to function.

My typing failures occurred in the morning, and my other failures took place while attending afternoon clerical report classes. At first, the forms were quite simple, but soon they looked more like the IRS income tax forms of the day. These complex forms annoyed me so much that I deliberately shifted mental gears over to the other side of my brain and went for the creative, artistic challenge that lured me to fulfillment. My urge to draw soon overtook the desire to listen to the instructor. I found my pencil and private sketch pad taking me into another world. The experience was so restful and therapeutic, compared to the mental torment created by the jungle of confusing paper work. I drew nature pictures with trees, mountains, and plants.

After several days of artistic pleasure—never detected by the instructors—I was becoming aware of how far behind I was. Shortly, the reveal-all testing day came, with typing skills first. I gave it my best, but my 8th-grade typing class came back to haunt me. Twelve words a minute was my peak. That score was great compared with what happened next. I totally bombed out in the clerical exams. I scored a give-it-all-you've-got USC 0 again. Needless to say, the test results did not go over well with the bosses. These bosses were not the instructors, but behind-the-scenes review boards consisting of about five or six men of significant rank and authority.

Cautiously, humbly, I entered the board room and was promptly addressed by the lead man in charge. The other men, in absolute silence, glared at me. I realized that this situation was much different from the one at the helicopter school, where I had been given kind advice by only one officer.

This time, I was surrounded by very troubled, suspicious, powerful men, who were there to challenge me and get to the bottom of the situation. Staring me down, the lead man began to let me have it by verbally reading me off. It went something like this, "We have seen your test scores, and they are disgusting. You have not only failed, but you have scored so low that there could only be one reason why you have done so. I believe you know what that is. Before you attempt to respond though, I'd like to remind you we are aware that not only have you succeeded in graduating from college, but you have also graduated from helicopter transmission school. Now, blankety blank give us an explanation for this failure stuff."

Meanwhile, I was in serious private prayer with God. I knew I was really in a pickle and needed to provide a quick, good answer. Well, somehow God disarmed the powder keg of anger as I began to speak. I humbly explained by first acknowledging my college successes, etc. and then began to attempt to explain my creative mental makeup. I told them I was an artist and didn't function well in non-artistic ventures, especially when difficult military pressures were hammering me. I told them that the typewriter noise threw me into such confusion that I was unable to concentrate. As I spoke, most of the guys began to let their anger down and allowed me to see more of a come-on-now look. The head man, however, never changed his angry look.

My best description of this look is to refer to the 1930's King Kong movie. If you can remember the giant King Kong gorilla and his eyes, then you will have some idea of what this guy looked like while he was eyeballing me. Not only did the head addresser look angry, but I felt that he was about to eat me alive, all the while rolling his eyes at me. He really let me have it by accusing me of being a shirker and warned me of the consequences should my actions continue as in the past. He said, "If you are called into such a meeting again, you will wish you never set foot on this fort. We have ways of dealing with people like you, and if you know what they are, you will surely understand then how we respond to shirkers. Go back to class and give more than a casual try."

I left these disciplinarians while trying to gather my thoughts. I knew I was in deep trouble because these men meant business. Their threats were real, and I knew that they could back them with action, believing I truly was a first class shirker. I also knew that I wasn't one, but I couldn't handle what was expected of me. With these thoughts, I chose once again to go to the Lord for help. As I spoke to Him, I rehearsed the past victories through which He had brought me. I remembered the escape cracks that He had always provided. He knew as well as I that I needed another one. I felt as if I was Moses backed up against the Red Sea and waiting for it to part so he could escape the enraged Egyptian soldiers.

In this hopeless state, I cried out for help. I knew that even if I gave the class work a gallant effort, I'd inevitably jam up and head in the same direction I had been before. Realizing this, I decided to do the only thing I knew to do and that was to wait for the Lord to open another escape crack.

Here I was in battle, once again, battling with the Lord's help. I became overwhelmed by the same problems, giving the typing and clerical work my best efforts. I even put away my sketch pad. The same test failures repeated themselves and I was desperately heading downhill with no way out. To make matters worse, the guys in my class began to make me the big joke. I took it well, while they pecked at me with jesting criticism.

Like a wounded chicken being pecked to death by the healthy chickens, I repeated the negative stuff, wearing me down and causing me to cry out louder to God for help.

God was allowing me to be stretched by the onslaught of humiliation and seeming hopelessness. I wondered how long I could handle the stretch without a sudden snap. As the stretching became almost unbearable, I suddenly found the long-awaited parting of the Red Sea. It happened in a way that I never would have expected.

Chapter Twelve

A Good Break

One day, while we were all in formation, it was announced that we were to be given more than the usual 15-minute break but, to our great delight, we were given a three-hour break. We couldn't believe it. Deals like this just don't happen. We were told that we could do as we pleased for the next three hours, explaining it something like this, "You sorry looking babies have the next three hours to pick up cigarette butts. So make sure you do a good job. Now, go for it."

Taking off quickly across the desert floor, I headed off to where—I didn't know. I cherished the free time as I was able to really have a heart-to-heart talk with the Lord. While walking and praying, I made a half-hour journey across vacant desert fields. Off in the distance, I noticed a rather unusual looking building on the fort; it was made of brick, rather than wood. Approaching it and getting a real close look, I noticed a sign out front with the words, "Craft Shop." Reading the sign, I said to myself, *Oh boy, an art shop; that's my kind of place. I'll check it out.* As I walked in, I noticed a bunch of ladies making ceramic objects from slip molds. As an artist, I was instantly aware that this was not real creative stuff. But, the ladies seemed to love it as they gathered in little fun social groups, talking trivia while putting final Mona-Lisa touches on their cherished treasures. I roamed casually through this rather large shop, noticing a hallway leading to the back of the shop. I decided to venture down the hallway and explore the unknown territory. Doing so, I noticed the hallway opened up into a series of art rooms, which turned out to be an artist's paradise. There were rooms with painting easels, various paintings hanging partially finished, and totally finished paintings hanging on the walls.

The rooms were very quiet so that no one could be seen in any of them. Browsing, I took great delight in thinking, *This is my kind of place.* Then, I heard a low roaring noise in a small room adjacent to the painting room.

Out of curiosity, I decided to take a little peek. There was a pretty lady in her late 40's spinning a clay pot on a potter's wheel. I could tell by the way she confidently handled the clay that she was an advanced potter. Noticing me entering the room, she lifted her head slightly and made a gesture and comment of kindness. I responded positively about her work, and before you knew it, we were talking art talk. As we found common ground in art talk, she continued to seize every moment in managing her clay in a masterful way. When her pot was turned to perfection, she stopped, gave me full eye contact, and said, "I can tell by your talk that you love art. What's your background?" I filled her in on all the art past: teaching, one-man art shows, etc. Then, she became very serious, took her attention totally off her own work, and made a quite refreshing statement, "We need someone with your experience and background to teach art at this craft shop." As she said this, my faith and hope wheels began turning fast. I responded by elaborating on my art interests and continued to tell her a little bit about my difficulties in functioning in my military-assigned, non-artistic duties. I said, "I am really having a hard time handling the clerk school."

"I'm in my own artistic world," she said. "I understand; we artists often are that way." Then, she said, "Why don't you give me your name and serial number and I'll see what I can do."

After giving the information to her and making some more small talk, I left with her words ringing in my ears, "You'll hear from me soon."

Many thoughts raced through my mind. I strongly suspected that God, once again, was in the process of delivering me from certain doom. I was convinced that my unusual encounter with the fellow artists was a match put together in heaven. I wondered who this artist was and why she had so confidently taken my name and serial number. It seemed that her action to do so said a lot without saying much. To me, it said, "Just watch what I can do."

These thoughts spun through my mind for about two minutes as I made my way out of the craft shop. Curiosity concerning the mystery of her identity got the best of me. I wanted to know who she was, so I casually made my way to the head desk and asked the crafts attendant who the lady was in the back room. She said with a smile, "Oh, don't you know who she is?" She is the Post Commander's wife, and she runs this fort. Whatever she wants, she gets."

I just stood there, speechless and in a state of elated praise to God. I said silently, "Thank you, Lord. You've taken me right to the top and put me face-to-face with the 'King's' wife."

Very soon, I was to learn that the King's wife or the "Queen", named Maxine, had been a World War II Woman's Army Corps Major. With her rank and experience, she knew well how to take command, even of her husband, I think. I won't say that her power had gone to her head, but I will say she was a very nice lady who knew what she wanted and made sure nothing stopped her if she felt her desires were righteous. Momentarily, I was to find out that she considered helping me as a righteous cause. I am not sure, but I think she began to think of me as sort of a temporary, adopted son.

Well, surely God designed the plot that began to unfold in a very interesting way, after my encounter with Maxine.

After the three-hour break, I joined the other troops, and we marched back to class. I decided to keep my little secret tucked in my head. I wasn't going to let these chicken-pecking typists in on my secret. I decided to keep quiet and wait out this one. I didn't know at the time, but Maxine was already starting to pull strings behind the scenes on my behalf. She had all power at the local fort level and even some at the Pentagon level, I believe.

One morning, just after we had sung our good-morning wake-up song to the rising sun, I was called out of formation, without explanation. I was told to report to the fort Craft Shop for further instructions. Leaving my wondering buddies standing at attention, I made my way to the Craft Shop, where I was greeted by my new commander, Maxine. Here, I was ordered to get casual. Before I knew it, I was in civilian clothes, hidden under an official Craft Shop smock. After a first day of getting acquainted, I was back in the barracks to join my weary ex-classmates for evening fellowship and a good night's rest. Of course, there were lots of questions and lots of explaining to do.

Again, as in the past, after a big low—followed by a big high—I took the opportunity to do a little self-motivated ego boosting. This time, I really needed a high lift. Just like the old college days' elevator experience, playing the naive genius role to get the last laugh with the smart guys, I played a similar role. I waited for an inquisitive crowd to gather. Then, I said, "Well guys, the Post Commander's wife and I have become good friends, and she has determined that my non-clerical gifts are needed elsewhere. Yes, she has decided that the Army has enough paperwork handlers to use up their time. So, from now on, guys, I'm 'Private Artsy Crafty.'" In fun and laughter, I joked with the guys. Actually, I wasn't cocky. I didn't want to come off in pride, but wanted a sort of last laugh as I kept them guessing what this was all about. Most of the guys were quite baffled by the unusual circumstances and never thought of the outcome as anything more than a series of good luck coincidences.

Graduation from clerk school was fast approaching, and by permission of Maxine and the high command, I was on loan to the Craft Shop. Actually, as far as the Military was concerned, I was still preparing myself as a clerk. I will probably never find out what actually happened behind the scenes but, somehow, I graduated as a qualified Army Clerk.

Finalizing my graduation, I was called in by Maxine for a heart-to-heart talk. I knew when I saw her face that something negative was up. She got right to the point and said, "Ed, I have bad news, I've done everything I can to get you permanently assigned as an artist at this fort, but there are just some things that cannot be done. Pentagon orders are not easily changed." I thanked her for the kind interest she had shown by trying to help me. Then she concluded by encouraging me and assuring me that the next few weeks of my stay at the Craft Shop would be enjoyable.

Negative news implanted, I thought this didn't make sense. I didn't believe all the pieces of the puzzle were in place. Somehow, I just knew that the final puzzle piece, when put in place, would show the perfect total picture. Shortly, the mysterious lost puzzle piece came out of hiding. When it did, everyone, including the Post Commander's wife, saw a picture that only God had put together.

The puzzle piece was delivered to me as I received news from military channels that as a qualified Army Clerk, I was to be assigned to report to my next duty station.

The next duty station could have been anywhere in the world, including Vietnam. But by God's divine intervention, low and behold, it was my same present stomping grounds, a little known fort tucked away in the beautiful desert mountains just outside Tucson, Arizona, named, Fort Huachuca.

Being assigned as a clerk to this fort was most unusual. The news came as a real shock to my "Kelly Girl" buddies who were mostly given assignments in Vietnam. When I ran the news by Maxine, she was shocked too. First staring and then smiling, she said, "I want you to know that I had nothing to do with this. This is beyond me. You just seem to have good luck." (Silently, I knew differently; this was not luck, but design.) She went on to say, "Well, now that you are here, things will go well for you." I was to learn that she was telling the truth. As I said before, this lady had real power. If she wanted something at the fort, she had it. In fact, I remember one incident in which she wanted her old two-story Victorian style home painted, and decided that only officers were qualified for the challenging task. And guess what, only officers painted her house.

Things began to change immediately for me. The usual early sunrise was exchanged for the sleepy head 9:00 A.M. rise. This caused quite a stir one morning as I slept in long after others were performing their duties. One morning, while I was rolling over to catch a few more Zzzs, I was awakened by curt, sharp remarks of an inspecting officer. As he flipped his lid when observing my peace and comfort at such a late hour, he demanded immediate response and explanation for my behavior. I humbly replied from my nervous position that I was an artist working with Maxine. After a brief stare and pause of reflection, I was aware that nothing more needed to be said. The very mention of and association with the name, Maxine, said it all. With a quick, "At ease, at ease; carry on, carry on," the officer drifted from my presence. This was the most positive encounter I had yet.

My usual daily duty involved instructing various military personnel, as well as their families, on how to do many types of art work. Of course, when no one showed up, I was free to express myself artistically as I saw fit. This turned out to be quite a fulfilling experience.

Chapter Thirteen

The Way to
San Jose

After I had several weeks of this good life style, Maxine decided that I and two of her other "kids" should join her on a trip to San Jose State College, to attend a crafts seminar. Of course, this would be considered special TDY (Temporary Duty) and would require extra pay, with special travel benefits added. After careful planning, four of us headed out in my green Chevy across the desert. Our first stop was Riverside, California. Here, all of us had dinner and spent the night at my folks' house. From there, we headed through Los Angeles. Since I had the urge to visit my old buddy, Dennis the Mole, at USC. I convinced Maxine that we should hold over in the USC area for a day or so. She agreed, and we got two motel rooms right next to the USC campus.

I was just about to find out that you couldn't cross Maxine, and I was about to have a jolting experience that I will never forget. After breakfast together, I asked Maxine if it would be all right if I took off with the Mole for a while, to see old sights in Hollywood, etc. She consented. For you to have insight into the craziness of what was to occur next, I must sidetrack long enough to inject some factual history concerning my long friendship with my old buddy, the Mole.

Since our early days as best friends, Dennis the Mole and I were notorious for bungling things up in a colossal way, whenever we got together. We were like two Laurel and Hardy or Abbot and Costello clowns attempting to function normally when asked to perform simple tasks. To make matters worse, we both had artistic temperaments. One revealing experience that tells the disastrous team-up story the best took place at a high school Young Life Camp in British Columbia. As chosen members of the elite summer work crew, we were singled out as the perfect team to perform certain duties. This decision turned out to be a costly mistake.

Early on, it was noted that everything we touched had failure written on it. When given the job of building a basketball hoop backdrop, we measured wrong and made it 6 feet long and 2 feet high. When using the wrong glue on dining room chair legs, we saw 14 people end up on the dining room floor during one meal. While performing kitchen duty, a tray of delicious hot sugar rolls accidentally fell on the floor, unnoticed by the head cook. Some breakfast campers screamed as they discovered compressed mop strings embedded on the bottom side of their rolls.

Then the all-destructive event that provided us with an early exit from work duty happened when the work crew boss foolishly trusted us to transport a large glass bottle filled with highly flammable photographic acid. It ended up broken on a burning boardwalk. I could go on and on and on in order to make it clear that, truly, when the two of us were put together, we were a double disaster waiting to happen.

Maxine said, "Sure, guys, go ahead and take a day together and just have fun. I'll just relax the day until you return." She had no idea what her involvement would be. With her approval and permission, off we went in the Mole's yellow Mustang to see old sights in Hollywood. After one of the crazy Mole tours, requiring multiple stops at various shops and memorabilia zones, we realized that it was getting quite late.

In usual style, we needed a couple of more hours so we could indulge ourselves in pleasurable visual "cocktails." That move turned out to be a serious mistake, as the blind Mole got lost on a sure thing, quick short-cut home. By the time we finally made it back to Maxine's motel room, it was very late, and I was extremely nervous. I approached her door, knocked, and then she answered. I didn't recognize her; she wasn't the Maxine I had known. This time she was the 1943 WAC Major in command and very upset. She immediately announced to us that we were AWOL and that her husband had been informed of our actions.

Well, I did a little prayer. After eating humble pie, she calmed down and, suddenly just as if nothing had happened, she was on the phone with her husband informing him that her prodigal sons had returned home to Mom. After this educational experience, I knew never again to make this kind of mistake. Next morning, we took off for San Jose. The crafts seminar turned out to be a great experience lasting several days. Later, we were really up in spirit, feeling refreshed, and enjoying the trip home, except for a leaky gas tank. But, all turned out well.

The next few months, my fellow Craft Shop workers, Jim Oaks, and I visited Maxine at her home so we could see all of her art work, which consisted largely of her beautiful ceramic creations. On one occasion, she had the two of us over for a special first-class dinner. I remember the large, elegant table being set with various choice dishes. The setting reminded me of a scene in the movie, *The Sound of Music,* when the stern baron sat at the head of a long, perfectly prepared table. In this case, the baron was the Post Commander. He was a Humphrey Bogart look-a-like and never said a word. His silence made me uncomfortable and quite nervous.

As the Commander sat in meditative silence, his unexpressed thought leaked out. He seemed to relay that he was having us as guests only to pacify Maxine's mothering instincts. In doing so, he managed just to tolerate her whims. Maxine made sure we were well fed and satisfied. Although I greatly appreciated her kindness, I was relieved to depart the strained scene as I never seemed to get used to being around high-command officers. I was always afraid I'd bungle something.

Much more could be added about my unusual, fun experiences at Fort Huachuca. After several months stay at the fort, I had a continual, rather troubling thought lurking in the back of my mind. This thought was, *How much of this 24-month time of required service had been eaten up in order to keep me out of Vietnam?* Approaching the glorious half-way point of one year, I was alertly aware that if I made it to one year and one day, I'd never be sent to Vietnam. It was a well-known, much-talked-about fact that the Army didn't send troops to Vietnam for less than a 12-month period. They considered it too costly to do so. So, I was quite excited as I met the 11-month mark, with no orders for Vietnam yet.

I was counting off the days when, suddenly, I was called to report to the sergeant's office. I began suspecting the unthinkable was about to happen. The sergeant told me to sit down and brace myself for what I was about to hear. He said, "Bowen . . . (pause), you've got orders to go to Vietnam . . . (pause)." This said, my already pounding heart began to have a real workout. I was shocked when I heard the "V" word and thought, *Lord, please let there be just one more crack to slip through.* Praying this, my mind quickly became aware that the Army considered me a qualified helicopter door gunner. I thought, *Well, "D" Day for me has finally arrived.*

My suspected, fearful thoughts were quickly adjusted as the sergeant asked me to further brace myself for the next words. Heart still pounding and my full attention given, I heard the most liberating and unusual words imaginable. The sergeant said, "Bowen, I've been in the Military for almost 20 years, and I've never seen orders like these." He paused and readied himself for the next poignant words. He stated, "Bowen, you have gotten orders to go to Vietnam, but you don't have to go if you don't want to . . . (pause)."

These words uttered, I dropped my quivering lips—almost low enough to keep beat with my pounding heart. I was speechless, and so was he. After regaining my composure, I said, "What do you mean, I don't have to go if I don't want to?" He said, "Well, it will need a little explaining. It seems that someone in a high position has selected you for a very choice volunteer assignment as a combat artist. As a military artist, you will travel all over Vietnam for three months, taking reference photos and making sketches and paintings of various military operations. After you have gotten a good feel of the area, the Army will then escort you to a safe, secure environment, more conducive to allowing your creative skills to flow with ease. They have chosen the *jungles* of Hawaii as that location."

All this said and orders given, my quivering lips were now laughing lips. I said, "You have got to be kidding me!"

He answered, "I'm not joking; as I said before, I've never seen military orders presenting such a deal to even the most high-ranking, respected, dedicated military men. I don't know why they have selected you for this assignment, but one thing I know for sure is that you would be crazy to turn down such a deal." After that, he told me that my studio in Hawaii would be used to create artwork which would be used to record the war for historical, as well as, artistic purposes. He said, "Since the Vietnam War has begun, only a handful of men have been selected to perform such a duty." He then added, "I need to warn you about the obvious risks of such an assignment, but I will also say that truly the opportunities afforded you will greatly outweigh the risks."

As our conversation progressed, I flashed back to the time I'd done artwork for the sergeant at the helicopter school. I remembered my artwork slides that the First Sergeant had taken with him on his frequent trips to the Pentagon. I recalled the massive multiple golden stripes that had wiggled almost all the way down his arms and the fact that even lifer officers respected and looked up to him. Now, I was aware that surely six months earlier he had gotten the ball rolling. It had taken that long for the good results to take effect.

Interrupting my thoughts, the sergeant said, "You've got just one week to make your decision." I left his office in an awe struck state. Of course, I thanked the Lord for providing another escape crack for me.

I began contemplating the dangers of such an experience and started to get nervous. I thought, "If I go to Vietnam, how will I react when I come face-to-face with the inevitable, horrible consequences of war? Will I be able to handle it? If I get in a perilous pickle, will God let me escape as he has done in the past, or will He allow me to become a maimed or crippled soldier in His Army, to be used for testimonial purposes."

The next couple of days conjured up many mixed feelings about going to Vietnam. Wrestling with the matter, I got another Dear John letter from Ginger, the special girl in my life. Our romance repeatedly went back and forth from break up to reconciliation. The timing was perfect. I felt set free to go. After a few phone calls home, I made my much counseled and prayed-through decision, I decided to go.

It was time to say good-bye to Mom Maxine and the Crafts Shop crew. Maxine was very excited for me. She wanted one of her boys to be fulfilled in the artist's dream of creating—unhindered in an Hawaiian paradise. Leaving and departing was not an easy scene. The Fort Huachuca art gang had become a little family by now. We had experienced so much together in art ventures. We had built kilns together, talked art, compared paintings, analyzed scenes and renderings, and it was suddenly over. I was facing a new world of the unknown.

Chapter Fourteen

Vietnam

Time for a short leave allowed me to say good-bye to my family and friends, and I was off to Vietnam. In 1968, Vietnam was not a nice place to be. I distinctly remember the arrival in Saigon. Right off, the first thing I noticed, apart from the unusual scenery, was the foul odor that permeated the air. I realized, then, how privileged I had been to have grown up in a country with running water and sanitary sewage systems.

Joining the new arrivals who stepped off the plane, I made my way down a long ramp, past many guys who were standing, patiently waiting for us to vacate the airplane so they could board. These guys had just finished the required 365-day tour of Vietnam and were still in one piece. Their time of trouble was over, and they were heading home, for good.

Staring at us, many of them could not resist the desire to make sarcastic comments directed toward us. Negative comments that reflected the basic attitude toward the Vietnam War pounded away at our arrival.. Specifically, their one-liners showed us that patriotism had very little to do with this war. Their comments did not reflect an attitude of comradeship and were not encouraging to their fellow soldiers to have a single-minded attitude. Instead, these comments reflected cynicism, hopelessness, and despair.

Continuing down the ramp, dressed in our freshly-pressed uniforms, we heard phrases such as, "You poor sucker. You cherry. Have fun for the next year!" Stinging remarks given with expressions of superiority. They expressed themselves as King of the Mountain, with us new arrivals at the bottom.

Certain significant highlights stood out in my mind as I entered the combat artists' tour of Vietnam,

I dubbed us the "Picasso Patrol," our five-man artist team. The formal name was actually "Team 7." We had the clear purpose of rendering artwork that was to serve as an historical record of the war. This work was to become part of the Army's permanent War Art collection. We were given free reign as to the style and content of our artwork. To accomplish the task of producing the best art possible, we were required to experience all aspects of the war. We needed to see everything from combat action to cultural sights, so that we could feel, firsthand, both emotions, as well as thoughts of the native Vietnamese and our military men. Hopefully, this could be accomplished without getting wounded or killed.

The familiar phrase, "There are no atheists in fox holes", and I believe there are no pacifists in fox holes, either. When the enemy is coming for you, you are ready to fight back. When a mortar took out our out-door hole-in-the-ground toilet, 20 yards from my tent, I thought of the night before when all patrons were at peace there.

Later mortars hit previously safe zones that now became forbidden ground for seasoned chopper pilots to land. The Viet Cong now surrounded the fort with the intent of soon conquering it.

Few hid their feelings of terror as mortars began pounding the ground like giant foot steps. Desperate cursing filled the air as bombardment continued. This couldn't have been worse than the German Wolf Pack Submarine crewmen faced as they were spotted, targeted, and struck repeatedly with depth charges. Our vessel, however, was not a sub but a grass hootch. Mortars shook the ground, sending us almost airborne, as metal fragments ripped through the shack as if it were paper.

I low-crawled to a French-built swimming pool with crude, thick wall showers. Our perimeter held that night. The next day I learned of the Viet Cong's previous success at that very spot before we landed—a night of horror to remember. The North Vietnamese drugged soldiers assaulted the barbed wire perimeter and broke through strategic spots concluding in hand-to-hand battle. Relief couldn't get in, and no one could get out. This whole event ended with naked, shredded bodies of the Viet Cong draped over the barbed wire fencing due to land mines and machine gun fire barrages.

Gratefully, I was immediately whisked away by helicopter and headed for a new zone. By chopper, jeep, and tank I was taken through suspicious villages over the mountain and to an airport terminal. There were times of rest, however unbelievable, where the bottled coke became heaven of the moment—the eye of the storm.

The coke rests remind me of one of the combat artists in the background of my paintings, showing one of these peaceful scenes. The artist, in particular, was one who hung out of a single prop plane, dangling by his secured feet while he was head-first snapping photos of the ground war. The pilot almost lost it, the plane, and the artist with the shock of seeing his passenger in this position. We all wondered if the photographer had fallen, would he have thrown up the film back into the plane before plummeting into the war zone just to save the film.

CocaCola and beer were the main staples of refreshment in Nam. Beer, however, was the preferred drink. All kinds of beers were represented there. Coors would have made a bundle if a pipe line had been laid from the Rockies, through the Pacific Ocean, to the nether regions of the Nam war zones. Instead of their former breakfast of champions Wheaties®, beer became breakfast, lunch, and dinner for many a guy in the hot jungles. The pain killer whiskey of the Civil War was chosen by others. Drugs, however, got into the camps illegally from Thailand, and many became users.

The artist operation ran from base camp in Long Binh, next to Saigon, to where our private living quarters and studio were. After several days of orientation, each of us was armed with a .45 pistol for protection. We were asked to practice in the surrounding jungle.

After readying ourselves with orientation and pistol use, we ventured out—our goal of experiencing and seeing all that we could from the Delta to the DMZ. Armed with pencils, cameras and, of course, a disencumbering .45 pistol, we headed out on a C-130 aircraft and various choppers.

I soon found that we were entrenched in a first class operation, with top priority consideration. Fort Commanders, Colonels, and other high-ranking military personnel greeted us, treating us like kingly ambassadors. Our rank was not an issue, since for the most part insignias were removed. We were, however, identified by the distinctive words of "Combat Artist."

Being treated more like a peer, by high-ranking military personnel, I was greeted by the Commander upon arrival at his outpost and given a tour of the unit's operations. Often, after securing somewhat comfortable quarters, we were served a nice dinner, one prepared especially for the elite. On several occasions, I remember being seated at a table reserved for the highest in command, usually a Colonel or a Major. This treatment and placement actually made me feel very uncomfortable. Yet, I kept my cool and acted quiet and respectful.

In every situation, including eating dinner, I was prepared with my weapons—my open sketch pad surrounded by bullets, and my pencils. I was always primed to catch a Colonel in a positive, even heroic, pose. As soon as they saw me in action, rapidly scratching on my sketch pad, they made certain they held their position for an obvious overkill. I guessed they considered it their duty to ensure they were remembered for their part in history. They seemed to enjoy this personal art attention, and they wanted their units glorified in the same way. These experiences provided me with the opportunity of being treated with a little more class than the usual, private first class.

I gave these drawings my all, and truly enjoyed it. There were times when other matters, such as enemy attacks, caused me to lose enthusiasm. Being a lover and not a killer, I tried to avoid these combat instances as much as possible. Soon, however, I was to find out that the Vietnam War was a different kind of war.

Weary from Jungle Warfare

I used a reference photo when I painted this soldier. Jungle warfare took its toll on body, mind, and soul. This foot soldier faced the dangers of jungle warfare which included snakes, bugs, jungle rot, malaria, dysentery, leaches, mosquitoes, monsoons that drowned everything out but the pain and insomnia, and the ever-present threats of land mines and booby traps. The booby traps were devilish in design. A good one could turn a carefully plodding foot soldier into a wiggling shish kabob in a second. These traps took out body parts, feet, legs, arms, and sometimes the whole head.

I have painted a rendition of the Special Forces, the bravest of all the military. They headed out on impossible assignments. They are the keenest trained.

Combat Artist Team:

Top (from left):   First Lieutenant Jim, Private Ed, Civilian Advisor Fred,
                    First Lieutenant Roman

Bottom (from left): Specialist 4 Vic and First Lieutenant Tom

Tunnel Rat

The most dangerous mission in Nam was to search for booby traps and tunnel complexes holding all types of surprises. These were the gutsiest soldiers of the military since they faced the unknown demolition material. The choice when entering a tunnel was either to hear "clear" or an explosion. Rats could find incredible surprises of entire cities underground with networks of hospitals, munitions factories, command centers, weapon caches, etc. Sometimes the rats were trained dogs instead of military men.

Poised for Battle

The soldiers here have been painted shown in conflict with the Vietnamese. This photo depicts the intensity of the moment of battle. The soldier on the right is very young, one of the many who faced the war of futility.

Rejection

I painted these soldiers as they faced rejection when a full "chopper" couldn't take any more. One out of four was killed or wounded in this battle, yet they had to go back for more. On returning home, they faced the rejection of war protesters in a country divided.

Trapped and Drawing Fire

I used a reference photo when I painted these men drawing fire. The men comprise two Americans and one South Vietnamese. The solders were trapped in a bomb crater, waiting for a "chopper rescue." Reports have been made of rescuing choppers brought down in their mission into bomb craters, where the wounded waited to be freed. As the chopper attempted a landing, it took a hit and landed where the wounded waited, inflicting further injury and death.

Looking Back
Here I have captured a soldier who contemplates the reasons for being where he is, the purpose, and what lies ahead.

Entering Nam

Wasting a Human

Just another dead "Charley" to the U.S. Military. Just another expendable pawn to the NVA Army Command. An eternal heartbreak to his family. An unknown to the U.S. soldier that had to stop him. Yet, to God, he was a much-loved creation, one for whom He sent His Son to die.

Crossing a Jungle Stream

Description of Painting: I have painted one of the riskiest maneuvers of war—crossing a jungle stream. If a trip mine didn't activate then the leaches would get the soldiers. Americans wised up and learned to used Charleys as human mine detectors in these dangerous waters. If Charley made it through, then OK, if Charley died trying, then others were saved.

Peace in the Storm

My painting—a rare rest period from battle. Coke® was a luxury drink during hard times.

Left to right: My sister, me, and my mom. Emotions were running high just before leaving for Nam. They wondered if I would ever return home in one piece.

Right inset: Ginger and me—my "Dear John" Ginger.

Here I am pictured after winning the silver medal for second place swimming race. At my left is the first place winner, John. From then on, second place was my usual position, because Dave Thompson always won the gold. The photo was taken at the Riverside Mission In swimming pool at the time Disneyland was having its grand opening. This was the buff me when I had those long conversations with Sandra Jennings all the time.

Mom and Dad—the regal couple.

Grandma Marie waiting
for her uncle's visit to
America.

My grandmother told her own stories about
her Welsh uncle who gave her a first-time
visit. Due to the excitement of his visit, he
wanted to take the fastest transport available, transport with low fare for the steerage passengers. He chose the Titanic. As
later discovered, a meager few from that
class made it. He was one who did not!

Uncle Gordon   Uncle Bill   Mom   Dad   Uncle Norm

The United States and Canada are free today because of guys like these; laying down their lives to resist oppressive governments.

Great Grandfather
Charlie   Great Uncle Joe   Uncle Len   Uncle Dunc

Grandfather Ed   Me, Ed   Uncle Jack

Generations of War

No exception, my family, too, was involved with the centuries of wars. Each has his story to tell, but not all made it back to tell it.

Gord—Gord was the oldest of four brothers, and resisted Hitler as a tank crewman. He was the silent type, but broke silence one time to tell of war horror that gave him nightmares for life. He watched his best buddy stick his head out of a tank and take a direct hit from a nazi round, leaving only his neck showing.

Bill—Bill was 6' 6" tall and a good target for the nazi warriors. He took several rounds to the body with serious shrapnel wounds leaving him suffering for years. All the cousins considered Bill a hero. After World War II, in the '40s, Bill became a Toronto policeman. We remember the front page article of him carrying a feisty, resistant woman as if she were a rag doll. He lost his battle with painful wounds early in life when he died from the results of these wounds. He was the son who found his father dead, early in life, leaving my Dad's family fatherless at a young age.

Mom—Her time in war was served in keeping the family together in daily pursuits. She fought for every righteous cause that crossed her path. Then she went to war on the golf courses and won.

Dad —He served time in the Royal Canadian Air Force for World War II. He has become successful not only in his business ventures, but also as a great father and husband.

Uncle Norm—He was 17 years old when he was involved with the Western Europe clean-up act of World War II. He is a successful Canadian businessman whose company has branches in Germany today. How ironic! He has always been the baron type, much like the one in *The Sound of Music*.

Great Grandfather Charlie—My great grandfather fought in the Boer War in South Africa, in the 19th Century. He carried many war stories with him into the 20th Century.

Uncle Joe—To many nieces and nephews, Uncle Joe was one of the greatest heroes as he fought in the trenches of France against a young Corporal Hitler in World War I. He lost a leg, took mustard gas, and swelled up like a balloon, succumbing to the effects of the gas as a young man. The London Gazette (9/7/1917) cited Joe Summerbell: "For conspicuous bravery and devotion to duty in attending to the wounded under heavy artillery and machine gun fire. He, no doubt, saved many lives, he remained out in 'No Man's Land' for several hours searching for wounded. He has previously done very good work in bringing our wounded in from enemy trenches during raids."

Uncle Len—Other photos show my Uncle Len who flew in India during World War II. His missions were known as suicide assignments. Needed supplies had to reach cut-off troops. Uncle Len flew supplies into them. Three out of four lifts made it. His didn't make it, which left my cousin, Wayne, fatherless.

Uncle Dunc—My Uncle Dunc was a recon photographer of World War II. He took some of the documentary pictures of Beltzen Concentration Camp in Germany—yet another war artist.

Grandfather Ed—My grandfather Ed, like me, was a lover and not a killer. He was assigned as the High Command General's Librarian in World War I. He loved to read. Later he owned his own business as an artist lithographer after the military.

Me—I've already explained the many facets of me and the Vietnam War. My father's sister, Aunt Marg, always encouraged me to press on in my art. As a result, she had a major role to play in keeping me alive in the Vietnam War.

Uncle Jack—Uncle Jack was another war hero, a Royal Canadian Air Force Pilot. He flew the English Channel to clear the skies of the German Lufthofa Mission against England.

While our family men were at war, the wives, sons, and daughters waited hopefully to not receive a "letter of regret." Only Marg, Len's wife, received the dreaded letter.

Casualty of war hits all those involved, even if it is the enemy's side. Families hurt and their hearts ache from casualties as well as death. How must the German families have felt when they had word that their husbands, brothers, nephews, and uncles were frozen to death on the fences at the Russian front? Did Hitler care?

But the war of times continues, not only on land, but in the spiritual realms, as well. The greatest war is the one that continues without bullets, machine guns, atomic bombs, nuclear weapons, chemical warfare, tanks, planes, submarines, or aircraft carriers. The war between God and Satan—to see who will take the offering each extends—the greatest war of all time.

Youth 'Robs' Bank Legally

Eddie Bowen, 13, above, might be termed a legal bank robber. In the past few months he has gotten away with about $25.

Eddie, son of Mr. and Mrs. John G. Bowen, 4210 Maplewood, is a numismatist, or coin collector, who several times a week goes to Citizen's Bank to exchange dollars for pennies that might include a treasure.

He examines each roll of pennies for rare specimens, which he then keeps and exchanges for one-cent-value pennies before returning the rolls to the teller.

Here he is searching through $18 worth of pennies in hope of finding the rarest of all the coins, a 1943 copper penny minted in San Francisco.

Bing Crosby reputedly has offered a brand new Cadillac for such a coin, and Henry Ford II at one time was offering a new Ford for the same treasure.

So far, Eddie has found two rare coins, a 1914 Denver penny, and a 1909 San Francisco penny, each worth $12. Net gain to Eddie, $24. Who else can get away with that much from the bank for nothing?

Amazingly enough, Eddie, who has some 500 coins in his collection which he started four years ago, has a first Century copper coin worth only $1, less than his rare American pennies. But these old coins apparently abound in Greece. Nobody offered even a chariot for those.

Legal Bank Robbery
Ed Bowen: Pictured in the Riverside Press Enterprise, front page, July 25, 1956

Girls, Art, and Teaching

BY POPULAR DEMAND: MR. BOWEN

By JENNIFYR GILMORE

The first thing I noticed when I met Villa Park's new first-year art teacher was the shocking baby-blue of his eyes. His healthy tan and pleasingly shaggy brown hair give him the type of look similar to that of an innocent naughty 11-year-old beachcomber.

To the accompaniment of the Kingston Trio, Mr. Bowen excused his long haircut with, "my barber just died." But looks tend to be deceiving and his intelligent, ready answers and opinions were clear evidence of a sharp, capable personality.

Mr. Ed Bowen, our pedagogue personality for this issue, has lived in Canada, Santa Barbara, and Riverside. He earned his bachelor of arts degree at the University of Southern California. He plans to continue his studies in order to obtain his masters degree. Art is his major and main interest. He minored in history.

Saying that he has been drawing for as long as he can remember, he gradually progressed from a classroom doodler to the winner of the "Most Outstanding Art Student" title during his sophomore, junior and senior years of college. He specializes in oils and has held two one-man shows in Riverside. Also, he won $100 in the 1964 All-California Art Exhibition held in San Bernardino.

Bowen described a perfect date as "the beach on a warm night, waves quietly breaking and no fire." Asked about his particular likes and dislikes as far as girls were concerned, he said that he disliked snobs and liked athletic, natural-looking girls with a sincere personality. He also explained that if he had to choose which of the two he considered more important, he would pick personality over appearance, al-

Mr. Ed Bowen looked in a mirror and came out with this self-portrait.

though he thought it a girl's responsibility to make herself as attractive as possible.

A good teacher is essentially, according to Mr. Bowen, an "effective motivator." He explained that he considers an avid interest in the subject and a desire to learn to be the two most important attributes in a good student. In discussing creativity, he said, "Everybody is potentially creative. Each person is born with creativity, but somewhere along the way they become insensitive."

Today's younger generation, as a whole, was described by Mr. Bowen as "deteriorating, living for the moment, searching, but headed in the wrong direction. The hippies are also searching, so they are really different only because they try new things in their search. In my opinion, they haven't found the answer."

He feels that the general lack of concern about religion found

today in the current younger generation along with the definite moral decline is a bad and discouraging sign, but he doesn't put the kids down. He says, "The reason they live for the moment is that they are desperate for answers."

This art instructor said "Villa Park is great. I love the area. I've found most Spartans to be interested and industrious students."

Self Portrait

This was printed when students called me Mr. Bowen. Two weeks later I was at the Cold One's desk. Four weeks later I was at Fort Ord.

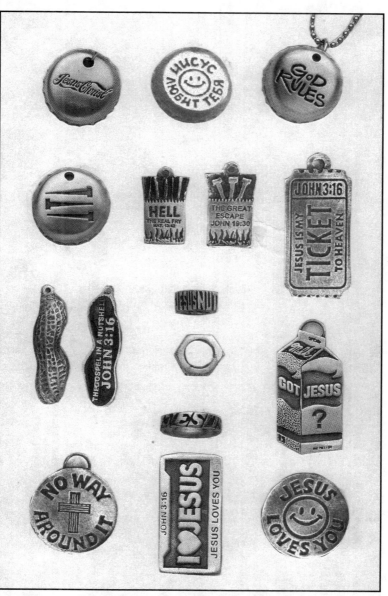

"Never make another piece of jewelry, huh?"

Me and "The Mole"—USC Fraternity Pictures

Left:
Dennis
Boucher

Right:
Ed Bowen

Middle left: A fifth-grade drawing of George Washington by Dennis Boucher

Middle right: A fifth-grade drawing of Abe Lincoln by Ed Bowen

Bottom: My first major art award "Bus Street"

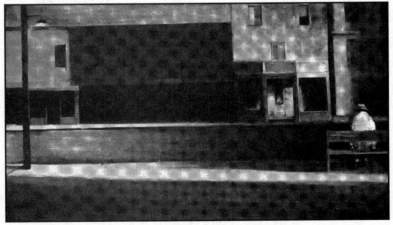

Dennis was the best artist I have ever known. He won so many First Prizes in California that he finally gave up. The USC professors really admired his work, and they passed him on the world's shortest thesis (1 1/2 pages)

Fountain Valley High School Students:
Top row: Left to right: Paul Olson, Sheri Roberts, John Conroy
Middle row: Left to right: Michelle Pfeifer, Karen Roderick, Ed Bowen

Villa Park High School Students
Bottom row: left to right: Christine Haase, John Meulmeister, Karen Scheblein

Smiling Karen sat in the front row in art class. John Muelmeister continues as
Art Department Director. Christine Haase shut off the music during my goodbyes.

Family Pictures
Polly—My former wife pictured in her last modeling photo.

My daughter, Susie Bowen

My daughter, Kelley Gilmer

Back Row: (Center) Ed Bowen • Middle Row: (fourth from the left) Mike Garrett • Front Row: (far left) Mike Garrett • Front Row: (far left) Ron Swary (fourth from the right) Earl Nitta. Ron Swary produced the Vietman TV series "Tour of Duty".

Paul Seiler

Unforgettable Faces and Game:

All remember the infamous USC/ Notre Dame Games Played in 1964.

God doesn't keep score, but He does enjoy games. The USC / Notre Dame game held everyone in suspense as *Time Magazine* advertised in their article that Note Dame was unbeatable. Evidently, USC hadn't read the article. Everyone in these photos were there that day. There were only seconds to go to game's end when a pass was thrown to Sherman in a tricky play. He caught the perfect pass to score the victory points. Pandemonium broke out in the L.A. Coliseum as never before and probably never since.

Paul Seiler remembers this game very well because he was on the Notre Dame side in Defense Lineman position. Paul went on to become a pro with the Jets and the Raiders, as well to play on the winning team with Joe Namath.

Today, Paul is a pastor and Mike Garrett is still at USC as the Athletic Director, after being a U.S. Congressman. He was formerly a Heisman Trophy winner.

Eddie, Polly, Ollie

A Spiritual General

Bill Peters—He goes into spiritual warfare daily and trained for combat. He lectures, preaches, and reaches people in practical ways, using the training he experienced in combat. He recounted the time when the chopper had made a drop and flew away as he and his other six men scurried for cover. The enemy of Nam passed them by only a few feet, yet they remained undetected. His assignment was to capture an enemy officer. The mission was accomplished with the enemy still alive. I was included in a dinner Oliver North attended, and I was invited to display my combat artwork at the dinner that evening.

My Sister, Sharron

Sharron—We were like two peas in a pod growing up. We were best buddies until she found out that all kinds of guys liked her. It was then she nicknamed me "bean brain." I used to peek my bean brain shaved head out of a "spy" window to watch her teach various guys how to kiss. She never knew I was there, but boy was it fun to watch. Her kissing didn't stop. At USC a lot of frat guys got real friendly with me when they found out that she was my sister. My dad chased a lot of the guys off when she was younger. Later, he gave me that job while at USC.

When Sharron was I7 and I was 16, she went to the Young Life Camp in British Columbia, called Malibu Club, and became a Christian. After that, she never called me "bean brain" again.

Today, she is happily married to a handsome Christian man named Ralph Buschman. My nephew, her son Marshall, is my only nephew in the family, and what a sharp young man!

Top: Sharron; Bottom Sharron and Eddie
(2 peas in a pod)

Dad in a magazine picture from the early 1940's

Dad - Every kid likes to look up to his dad - mine was ft. 3in. He was handsome to all the ladies in Toronto. His modeling pictures were plastered all over on billboards and magazines. I snuck this photo from his file that he had tucked away. Passing one of the billboards and catching a glimpse of himself he reflected that perhaps that face should be in pictures with Jean Simmons or Vivian Leigh. He probably thought, "Maybe I could even give Clark Gable or Errol Flynn a run for their money."

I was only four when I heard the word "California" and it was repeated over and over. Before you knew it, we were all packed into our '47 Chevy and headed for the home of the stars. Santa Barbara was only a stop-over for my dad, a place to get recognized. Almost immediately, he was cast in the "Home of the Brave". He played the role of "Finch" at the Alhecama Theater. The Santa Barbara News (March 21, 1948) quoted, "John Bowen, who plays Finch, has taken many roles at the Toronto Civic Theatre and participated in the Dominion Drama Festival. He was a member of the Royal Canadian Airforce."

While playing another role, my mom, sister, and I went to see him. He was spotlighted, the theatre darkened, and silence fell. All of a sudden, this little blond-haired girl leapt to her feet and yelled, "That's my daddy!". I guess she stole center stage from him that day. The audience were broken up by her spontaneity.

His acting was great and soon the Hollywood scouts scoped him out and said, "You know he is just the man for the part in our movie "Home of the Brave". Although Dad's hopes were high, they faded when a new actor by the name of Lloyd Bridges got the part. Mom had different ideas of what part Dad should play, her emphasis was on his being home as a father to have fun with his kids more, instead of the theater. He phased out the acting role and took on the role of my first fishing buddy. Boy, did we have fun, especially on Stearns Wharf in Santa Barbara. After a good catch, we would head up State Street to catch one of those plays that Dad might have been in.

Although still an actor at heart, he kept the neighborhood kids entertained as they wondered what his role would be next. His part was the mean dad to Dennis who always chased my sister. To the rest of us, he was the mystery man. When our gang abandoned all else to race home and see Sea Hunt, I think Dad was really bugged—Lloyd Bridges got the starring role in that series—an American hero. The only role that surpassed it, then, was Davey Crocket, King of the Wild Frontier. At 84, Dad still acts as one of my friends found out the other day while feigning the old man role. After, he bounced up and left. My friend exclaimed, "He's really young at heart, isn't he?"

Viewing an early 1950's Billy Graham Crusade broadcast, as a young man, Dad made his decision to follow Christ.

My Mom/Golfing Group

Mom is seen here in the white outfit next to my golf hero Arnold Palmer. I am proud to put his picture here. As far as sports heroes went, he was only second to Mickey Mantle to us in Riverside.

My dad, my other hero, is the tall one on the right. He is a golfer, too—a retired one. His retiring hole was at the last hole on British Columbia's Gibson's course. Arnie would have said, "Wow," after popping one in the hole from 75 yards out. He quit when he was ahead and retired his driver (his club for all occasions, except for a hidden 9 iron and putter.) The other 17 holes at Gibsons will remain a secret.

Golfing was put to bed while we dragged out our fishing poles to catch a 9 and 19 pound salmon the very next day.

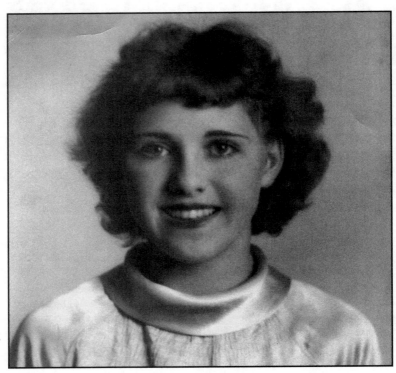

Mom as a teenager

Mom - What can I say about my mom; In one word, it would be "Fighter". The next word, "can't" will never be in her vocabulary. Mom's fighting is the admirable kind of fighting as she fought for causes not only in words but also in actions. She continues, and has always been, a leader.

Ever since I can remember, Mom was a president of this and that, from speaking clubs to PTA President, to President of the Golf Club at various locations as well as two different countries. The White House "throne" is probably the only goal she didn't go far because she was Canadian born.

The word "can't" signaled for her to go ahead and try. When I was five the word "can't" came up a the first phases of building a house from cornerstone on up. Never attempting this feat before and without prior knowledge of the blueprints and all, she forged on telling herself that this was not impossible. Mom learned how to do it all. When red tape and bureaucrats tried to block her way, they were flattened by her fortitude. Even the snag of blueprint delays couldn't stop Mom from forging on.

Mom is only 5' 4" tall, but that didn't stop Mom either as she was next seen cutting 2 X 4s with the hand saw and erecting walls. Would you believe it? Director was her next role as she guided plasterers, stone masons, roofers, plumbers, and electricians. Our house at 3425 Los Pinos Dr., in Santa Barbara, will never fall, believe me, nor will the other houses built in Riverside. None of the architects or builders in that city will ever forget Mom. They came from all over to check out her masterpieces and one architect complimented, "Only a woman could have designed this."

As a first grader, Mom's teacher mistakenly used the word "can't" when it came to her learning capabilities.

Not always a God-lover, Mom was a do-gooder with respectable goals, but once she picked up the Bible she gave the pages a good workout before becoming a full-fledged Christian. An old, rich drunk lady had much to do with Mom's conversion. Sitting in our living room, this lady with her rough voice told unforgettable stories of being wealthy, but without God. She only found contentment when she found her "real life" at the foot of the Cross. This lady's story, "The Late Liz", was only recently retold on "Focus on the Family" broadcast 40 years later—an awesome story.

The most predominant fighting "thing" occurred when I was 16 years old when I was 5' 5" tall and about 100 pounds. Mom said, "Eddie, you just keep quiet while I do all the talking." The Poly High School Vice Principal's office was soon to find out that Ed Bowen was a very intelligent young man. This dominating Vice Principal was extremely intimidating, but Mom was undaunted and disarmed him. He actually cowered to my PTA President Mom. What a lady! Reasoning was not the order of the day as he tried to convince her that I didn't have it "upstairs". Wrong! There was no argument. His bluntness paled my hopes as he demeaned me, while I reflected on my weak body that housed the "upstairs". Mom's demands urged my being placed in the advanced English class; and the next day, there I was as 30 mouths dropped by my presence. Boy, was I scared!

Even today, Mom fights on for noble causes as well as on the golf course—keeping up a fast pace.

Ed Bowen   Mike Napier   Dave Adler   Ron Schaffer

On call—heading for "Nam"

Painting of Vietnam backyard

THE GUYS - Our Gang
(Fifth Grade Class - Childhood Buddies)

Ron Schaffer (top row-third from left)   Lane Cash (second row from top-third from right)
Bonnie Weatherwax (third row from top-fourth from left)
Ed Bowen (first row-third from left)   Mike Napier (first row-fourth from left)

Senior Photos from High School

Mike Napier

Ron Schaffer

Dave Adler

Dennis Boucher

Ed Bowen

Lane Cash

Ken Rheberg

Bob Myers and Ed Bowen
Bob was a best man at my wedding.

Chapter Fifteen

Other Decorations
of War

Unlike the traditional wars fought by Americans, where there was pseudo safety for those away from the front lines, this was extremely different. A safe place one day was a perilously dangerous place the next day. Any helicopter seen by the enemy translated into a clay pigeon to the ambitious warrior. Travel in choppers was always very risky in Vietnam.

Other dangers in the Nam vicinity included snakes, bugs, jungle rot, malaria, dysentery, leaches, mosquitoes, monsoons that drowned everything out but the pain and insomnia, and the ever-present threats of land mines and booby traps. The booby traps were devilish in design. A good one could turn a carefully plodding foot soldier into a wiggling shish kebab in a second. These traps took out body parts, feet, legs, arms, and sometimes the whole head. At times, Vietnamese children were made into booby traps when assigned to give a GI a gift.

However, on the other side, some Charlies (Viet Cong) were thrown out of choppers when they became frozen in silence while under interrogation. I heard of one Charley who gave an obstinate look to his enemy officer and found a swinging machete headed for his neck. Certain Special Forces units had pride in displaying the ears of their enemies on their belts.

In the dark of night, a towering black peak pierced the sky like a volcano. This monster was considered a sacred place by the Vietnamese and a forbidden war zone to the Americans. This forbidden peak was a fortress that protected an American communications stronghold, secured by a shrine of barbed wire and then the shrine itself. The safest part of this spire was the top. Lingering in the lower regions of the mountain was an infestation of enemy activity with troops of moles burrowing in hidden tunnels, as the enemy tried to think of new ways to capture the peak. However, the top of the peak was the safest place in all of Nam.

But moles are never seen, usually, even while trying to peak. This gigantic cover-up camouflaged what was really happening. The truth is this mountain had Vietnamese troops honeycombing the base and upper tiers with their own surprises.

As I sat comfortably at the top, drawing the scenes of war, my awareness of the cover-up had not yet been realized. I learned how clear nights added to the security of the top. On foggy nights, however, the story could change to silent, surprise enemy attacks. The night was clear, when I lay down my sketch pad and went to my bunker. About midnight, I woke to the fog creeping into camp, a fog that thickened into soup, even hiding my hands from sight—a perfect time for enemy attack. The enemy moles were lurking in their tunnels, waiting to pop up in the camp and surprise our troops. Silence deafened our emotions but broke when my imagination conjured up digging noises nearby.

What a terrifying experience! This was the time when guys were grabbing their religious objects next to their dog tags and crying out to Mother Mary—a time when atheists were talking to the God they said didn't exist. It was a time when pacifists became intimate with their .45 pistols they previously wished weren't there. This was a time when believers begged to see God's face a little later in life. This was one of the longest nights in my life, bordering on terror. During my wait, I was told that our pioneer soldiers who went in envoy from the peak top, seeking to find just how safe the stronghold was, were never heard from again. Then, I heard the word, this peak was anything but safe.

However, the moles didn't strike that opportune night, and the next morning a chopper came to my rescue. Flying out and looking back, I wondered if the fog would roll in again and what the outcome would be—the mystery of war!

One Viet Cong, exhausted from his 500-mile trek through rough jungle terrain, followed his orders to deliver one mortar round designated for a destination in the south. But he gave himself up because his mission demanded that he turn around and repeat the trip for yet one more mortar round.

During the Battle of Hue, the Vietnamese who sided with the Imperialist Americans were lined up from oldest to youngest in families and systematically buried alive.

Frequently, while dwelling safely within the perimeter of a base camp, we would suddenly be hit by mortar attack. These attacks usually occurred on smaller base camps, some as small as one or two hundred troops. The bases were comparable to Cavalry forts, scattered across the badlands during the Indian wars of the 19th century. Inside, these forts were somewhat safe, with a perimeter of security guarding the internal central zone. However, unlike the Cavalry days, these Vietnamese forts were not made of wood or stone, but consisted primarily of barbed wire, trip flares, and mines nestled next to bunkers.

Mines were strategically placed about 50 yards apart, usually armed by two or three readied machine gunmen guards. At least one guard remained poised on constant alert and ready for possible enemy confrontation. Once in a while, the Viet Cong enemy would attempt to break through the fort's perimeter. If they succeeded, they could wipe out an entire bunker by providing a hole or entry point for masses of havoc-raising soldiers to enter.

If enemy soldiers entered, they attempted to take control of the fort. This would mostly lead to intense hand-to-hand combat, as fighting troops battled it out in the trees, bunkers, and buildings within the fort's perimeter.

This constant threat of attack, along with the inevitable, terrifying mortar and rocket attacks, would often bring fear and stress levels to boiling points. When a mortar attack occurred, the ground would pound and rumble. It would sound as if a huge giant was pounding large, deliberate steps on a path across the fort's terrain. If a rocket landed nearby, you could end up being a Killed-in-Action (KIA) soldier.

Pressures resulting from the threat of attack, as well as actual attack, began to get to me. I found myself putting aside my sand-jammed .45 pistol and grabbing my little black pocket-sized Gideon Bible. After being comforted with Scriptures, I usually pulled out my sketching book or write a letter home.

My Vietnam experience could be recounted endlessly. I remember, indelibly, my fears—the close calls and horrors of seeing the wounded writhe in agony as they tried to handle the excruciating pain of their torn bodies. Memories surfaced of compassion I felt for the hurting, lonely, hopeless, and frustrated troops. Even more as a visiting observer than a combatant, I was allowed to see soldiers' pain, while protecting myself, and not experiencing it. Often, I would feel guilty about my role. But seeing the wounded, maimed, and despairing captured enemy (Viet Cong) also made me hurt badly inside—a different kind of hurt and pain than theirs.

I remember looking into the faces of the many captured, seeing deep anger, and aware that much of their anger resulted from years, even generations, of warfare. One time, I saw a bus load of captured Vietnamese displaying their bodily wounds of missing legs, wrapped heads, bandaged arms. One girl was missing both legs. I saw these and other victims, as well, who were products of a mind-molding philosophy. This philosophy produced a controlling government that required its population to submit as expendable pawns to their government's conquering agenda.

Even knowing it was not my place to do so, I wanted to go up to those wounded ones and tell them that Jesus loved them. I wanted to say, "We can all get along if we all have Jesus in us." Although I never said anything to the wounded war prisoners, I did manage to pass out a few kind smiles, which said, "I know we are enemies, but I do care about you anyway." I never knew what effect such actions had on these people, but it made me feel good to contradict the confusion and hatred that seemed to consume these people. After thinking these things, I'll say that it's a good thing my basic training drill sergeant wasn't around to see that his attempts at instilling hatred in me had failed.

The majority of my Vietnam experience took place in crowded marketplaces and weird religious shrines. These places seldom were visited by GIs. Only after touring one of the marketplaces, I was warned by someone in the know that such a move on my part was crazy. He cautioned that risky actions on my part could easily leave me with a slit throat. I was basically naive when it came to war. Such foolish maneuvers on my part must have made my guardian angel work overtime.

Again, my compassion button was pushed as I witnessed the life-style of the primitive Indian-like dwelling Montagard people. These people had malnutrition, their children displayed the familiar swollen belly, alerting me to the fact that this world has its gross injustices. When drawing pictures of the very old and very young from this group, I was surrounded, almost engulfed, by them as they curiously watched me transfer their physical appearance onto sketch paper. I also recorded some of their strange, pagan religious practices on sketch pad, as well as on film.

After much travel, long waits in base camps, and traveling through the Vietnam villages, marketplaces, and large cities, I was intimately acquainted with the war, people, and land of Vietnam. Now, I was ready to head to the paradise called Hawaii where I painted, drew, and created other various types of artwork in a place free from the pressures of war.

Early 1969, I remember finally getting on a plane leaving Saigon with many immensely relieved and mentally, as well as emotionally-drained, free soldiers. These soldiers had done their time (365-day tour) and were finished with the war. A common euphoria of relief emanated among these passengers while we safely made our way out of the Taun San Neut Airport. Looking back through the windows of the airplane at Vietnam for the last time, we soon were dreaming of cool breezes, no dust or foul smells, just dreaming of Hawaii.

Our euphoria mushroomed into elation as we landed in Oahu. Quickly, we were escorted off to Schofield barracks, where we could see the filming of the *Tora, Tora, Tora* movie about the Japanese invasion of Pearl Harbor. How ironic; my Hawaiian experience turned out to be one of the most rewarding experiences of my lifetime. I call it my "Huck Finn" experience.

Chapter Sixteen

Huck Finn's Island

H awaii, what an idealistic time of escape for me. This experience reminded me of Huck Finn's island because, it was free from everyday hassles of uncomfortable people situations and stress. Pleasure came not only from freedom of pressure, but also because Hawaii provided a place of wonderful solitude and amazing beauty.

Even more pleasurable was the freedom I had in doing my much-loved art work—without the threat of strict military pressure and formality. The little pressure I did feel was the pillow pressing against my resting head after a long day's or night's rest, or the pounding of the powerful surf along the North Hawaiian Shore. Often I would take a day to escape into the luring surf for a break from long, creative painting binges. On this Huck Finn's island I was free from rockets and mortars. Except for close calls from falling coconuts, I escaped Hawaii unscathed.

We could let our hair down at Huck Finn's island. In Vietnam, I had become used to the longer-than-usual military haircut. I remember the four star General Abrams eyeballing me in an unusual way as I took reference photos of him in Vietnam. Although he never said anything to me, I think he noticed the longer hair and, for a split second or two, probably thought, *What's this Army coming to—a bunch of hippies fighting for our cause or what?*

In Hawaii, I got so carried away with artistic pursuits that I almost forgot I was in the military. There was no problem with this thinking as long as I wore civilian clothes and stayed cooped up in my painting studio. One day, however, I made a near fatal mistake. I wandered into dangerous territory while wearing my uniform. My hair was not only longer than acceptable, but also uncombed; my uniform may have been a bit wrinkled as well. This venture took me into a rather large officers' lounge and bar. I tried to sweep through a side door to go upstairs and set up an art exhibit.

Coming downstairs, later, I tried to make a quick escape. I hoped to move quickly enough to go unnoticed by the crowd in the officers' lounge. It didn't work. Surprise, out of nowhere, I was confronted by a serious military-looking individual. His head was beginning to turn beet red as he gave me a head-to-toe look. Drawing closer to him, I noticed that he had shaved his head to match his spit-shined boots. I don't think he had one hair on his head and, if he did, he made certain that it was cut so close that it gave him a Yul Brenner appearance or "Nair do" haircut.

Piercing angrily from his bull-dog-like head, were the most glaring eyes imaginable. Having my full attention, he immediately wasted no time in setting me straight. He snarled, "Soldier, how dare you allow that uniform to be worn in such an unkempt manner? Now police yourself up!" I responded humbly and nervously with an explanation. I told him that I was an Army artist and in the process of setting up an exhibit. Further, I explained that I had gotten a little dirty in the process. My excuse did not change his opinion of me. I was bracing for verbal abuse when suddenly one of the combat artists came to rescue me. The officer was able to soften up the situation a little. Finally, I left the incensed officer with little more than a firm reprimand.

I loved the tour on the island. Frequently, I painted all night or until early morning. Wearing T-shirts and jeans, I painted and painted, rested and rested and, of course, managed to wear my Bible pages out while enjoying the Hawaiian lifestyle.

Two or three months later in this wonderful, peaceful Hawaiian life, I waited for new orders. Then, I had to leave the island. I found that my tour in Vietnam was considered Temporary Duty (TDY) and, as such, I was still considered to be assigned to Fort

Huachuca as a clerk (in reality, a craft shop specialist). This meant that I would return home to Mom Maxine and the artist gang. Eventually, I could enjoy the comfort and beauty of the Arizona desert mountains, as well as have fun with all of my friends.

Arriving in Fort Huachuca, I was warmly greeted by Maxine and friends, finding myself in the same groove as in previous days. Except for a few of the old-timer craft shop family who had been sent off to Vietnam, the crew was performing as usual. All of us continued to indulge ourselves in the delights of talking and creating art. Excited, they all wanted to hear about my combat artist experience. As usual, Maxine was in the center of our fun.

I gave a slide show of 300 of my choice photos. The presentation was viewed with intense interest. Seeing my artwork blown up in slide form was quite rewarding to me, and I was left with a feeling of accomplishment. Maxine commented positively on my art, which gave me a lift, knowing that she both understood and appreciated the artwork. Following this special occasion, a new kind of respect seemed to be given me from my military associates too. My Private First Class rank was not even considered, now, as I related to all ranks.

At this point, I will say that even though I was treated respectfully, I still never could adjust emotionally to military life. I thought of it as a kind of prison. After almost two years of saluting officers, I was no longer aware that there were human beings behind those bars; they seemed more like prison bars than rank insignias. The thought of saluting those bars for five more months was almost more than I could bear. I longed to escape to civilian freedom.

Considering the frustration over being trapped in a military world that was so foreign to my nature, something unique happened to me again. I experienced something that forever softened my hatred toward all that is military. How could I imagine it would ever happen the way it did. When it occurred, I knew that the Author of such an experience had to be the One who had given me 30 units of As and Bs at USC. This time, however, the Author of undeserved awards really put the icing on the cake, when He accomplished this feat. Yet again, He made sure I was given an ego-boosting pat on the back after experiencing the depths of a crushed ego.

Chapter Seventeen

The Experience

One morning, I was in a large formation consisting of several hundred troops of various rank, when I was called out of formation. I was asked to come forward and stand silently, as I faced the rather vast crowd. On this occasion, I would have loved to have had the shirker-accusing military personnel present.

In front-and-center position and facing a most inquisitive crowd, a speech was being read for all to hear. The words baffled me. I knew I did not deserve them and, to this day, I don't know who was responsible for initiating and putting the speech together. I must say, however, I loved every word of it. As best as I can remember, It went something like this:

> Today, we are gathered here to give special honor and recognition to a soldier who served gallantly in special duty in Vietnam. He did this while experiencing the duress of intense and dangerous combat duty. He, with all courage and fearless effort, sought to bring honor to his country by volunteering for special duty. His efforts have truly and significantly, contributed to the betterment of not only the Army but the military as a whole.

(I don't recall hearing the word "art" or "artist" in this speech.)

Yes, he is to be honored and given appreciation by all of us here, today, for his efforts and contributions.

As these words were being spoken, I jokingly thought, *I wonder when he is going to pin the medal on me.* While wallowing in the glory of it all, my true thoughts were ones of thanks to the Lord for saving my crushed pride once again. Following a few more thick words, I was saluted and smiled upon by all. I need not tell you how puffed up I became as I returned back to formation position.

After dismissal, I was swarmed upon by curious, admiring peers. They wanted to know details, hear the whole story, etc. News spread and soon I made the Fort Huachuca papers. From then on, there was a new kind of respect shown to PFC Bowen.

A month later I learned that I was eligible for a three-month, "early out' from military service. To meet requirements and be eligible, I was required to guarantee pursuit of a college education. After applying, I was accepted, and soon I was doing the 30-day countdown and yelling the five-letter word, "SHORT!" Yelling this word was immediately recognized by all who heard it, meaning the one yelling it was a short-timer who would soon be released from military duty. This sound could be heard at any unexpected time, in unexpected places, and often was heard as an extremely loud shriek. It was heard in chow lines, showers, hallways, and even in the middle of the night when everyone was asleep. The shrieking sound was really not that bothersome to those who heard it, because it was thought of in a positive way. It was a signal that said that someday those hearing it would have their chance to yell it.

Another four weeks passed, then D-day arrived. In this case, D-day meant the day of departure from military life. That very day, my Chevy was packed with Vietnam-purchased cameras, reel-to-reel tape recorders, and all kinds of memorabilia. I also had a bunch of artwork strapped to the roof.

I dressed in casual, comfortable, civilian clothes and said my emotional good-byes to Maxine and the gang. Then I made my final exit and received my final salutes from the MPs at the gate. By the way, they saluted the car, not me, as my car somehow ended up with an officer sticker on it. (I never did figure out how that happened.) Somehow, though, I never got around to removing it. I just considered it another one of those God-given perks put there by my unseen Commander to let me know that I was spiritual officer material.

Off I went, a free man at last. As I drove away at dusk, I could see the lonely MP standing, silhouetted against the setting Arizona sun. At first, as I drove off, I was silent. This was probably due to the fact that for two years I had mental and emotional restraints imposed on me. As I drove in silence for a while, suddenly I burst into screaming and laughing and praising and singing. I must have gotten hoarse as I yelled my praises at the desert's rodents along the lonely stretch of highway leading to Tucson. When I arrived in Tucson, I grabbed some good civilian-cooked fast food and then headed for a motel. I spent an evening of meditative reflection on the awesomeness of my strange journey.

I began to think about the last two years, with all their ups and downs. My emotions had gone through a kind of tossing and turning. I saw them lifted to great heights, as the impossible turned into the almost miraculous. Then, I saw a spiral downward, to the deepest of despairing depths. These patterns repeated themselves until a virtual sequence of patterns sort of created a plot. I saw myself as a character in the plot put there by God for some purpose. I wondered why God was singling me out for such a journey. I wondered why I seemed to be fit enough for Him to save me and, at the same time, allow others to suffer and die. Pondering, I felt as if I had been wedged into a place where I was forced to trust in God. The whole process seemed to have led me into a preordained path.

Beginning to realize this, I certainly wondered to what kind of future the unseen guiding Hand would lead me. I wondered if I would continue on the up and down, crazy kind of road I had just traveled. I asked questions like, *Would I go back to USC, teach again, marry?* I thought about the past once more and the significance of July 16. It held one more treasure besides my birthday, it was the same day in history that saw men go to the moon. I considered the past pattern and was suspiciously aware that surely the future would be filled with more adventurously planned events, directed by the same One who had plotted and planned the dramatic past.

After meditating and getting a long night's rest, I headed for home, Riverside, California. There, I would reunite with my family and friends.

The first night home allowed me to reflect on the past once again. I remembered 21 months earlier I had wrestled with my feelings and was caught in the crossfire of trust and confusion. I reflected on the results that followed, when I finally laid down my thoughts and decided to just trust. I looked back on the results of that trust and saw they were good. It was obvious to me that all the goodness was given to me by God.

Wondering about this goodness, I decided to grab my old *Phillips* translation Bible that had been faithfully dusted off by my mother for almost two years, resting in its same spot, waiting for me to be welcomed for another visit. Before reading it, I glanced at the first page, which to this day has a short, almost forgotten, phrase on it. The words were dated and simply said, "God, how could you do this to me, allow me to be drafted?" Below, the words were written, "Look at this in two years and see what the Lord has done." As I read the phrases, I stopped, set the book down for a minute, and sat in stunned silence. I thanked the Lord for being so good to me. I thanked Him for letting someone as inadequate as me survive such an experience. I thanked Him for keeping me from what could have been a terrible experience and for turning it into a most rewarding and fulfilling one.

As I reflected on this, I was soberly made aware that, truly, God does care for all of us. Those who trust Him can dream big and see the Lord bring fulfillment to their dreams in ways that are beyond their wildest expectations. Truly, God does create some very unusual people. While others look down on them and even call them stupid, God has a different view of them, and He plans unique, wonderful experiences for these unusual ones. He creates, plans, guides, and schedules the very steps of these trusting souls. I know; I am one of them and I have seen Him do it.

Chapter Eighteen

True Escape—
A New Beginning

K ill, kill, kill was no longer an issue. My short tour in the Army was over, and I could pick up life where I had left it two years earlier. But for many, the war was still in process. Most from that generation faced a war in Vietnam, as much as they faced the war within themselves. For most, the Vietnam war was easy to figure out. It was kill or be killed. But the war within persons was not so easy to understand.

So many who suffered from the wounds of emptiness and loneliness left Vietnam, when the vacuum in their hearts never was filled in the way it was originally designed. These empty feelings took many on a search to fill the void with drugs, alcohol, elicit sex, etc. which didn't provide a lasting "high." Education, isms, asms, and spasms all failed them. Nothing could really satisfy the deep inner longing. To make matters worse, not only the purposeless and hollowness within them seemed to be heading nowhere, but the real Vietnam war was heading in the same place. There seemed to be no way out of the dilemma.

Amazingly, there was a way out, but few found it. Fortunately, I was one who *did*. The void in my heart was filled with what it was designed to be filled—with God. This is not something I say pridefully. The truth is, as a 17 year old, in 1960, I wasn't interested in

God, any particular direction in my life, a God plan, or even any meaning in my life. I was like most 17 year olds, mainly interested in doing my own thing. But, a message invaded my routine while at a Young Life Camp, in British Columbia. The message was so profound that it caused me to drop everything in order to let God be the Master of everything with which I was connected. This life-changing message I heard was very simple. It was a message that many in Vietnam would be familiar with only a few years after I heard it. It was a message about pain and battle.

The battle was not about pain and the suffering of fighting humans, man against man. No, the message was about the pain and battle experienced by God, as He fought in earth's arena for the only prize. This was for the souls of men, the weapon used was God's own body—in the form of Jesus. This battle had unbelievable pain, agonizing pain, and bloodshed. The pain of this War was no ordinary pain, a pain beyond anything man could imagine, and the blood shed was the blood of God, Himself, offered from a sinless Person.

The message was that of the cross and the suffering of Jesus. The message appeared profoundly dreadful but, in contrast, was the most glorious ever believed—God's good news. It was good for me, because of the battle won at Calvary. I could be connected to my Creator through the forgiveness of my sins.

The message told me that I was separated from God because of my sins, and God didn't want it that way, because He loved me. He wanted a change within me so that I could have fellowship with Him. The message told me that God wanted to bridge the gap between me and Him, a gap caused by my sin. I was told that His method of bridging the gap was the costly sacrifice of His only Son, Jesus, on the cross at Calvary. I was told that such an act was an undeserved gift given to me by the grace and mercy of God.

My response to the message was to receive that gift. When I did, the vacuum was gone, and the plan of meaning and purpose began to unfold. Seven years later, while in Basic Training, I heard the chaplain reiterate what I had become aware of when he said, "God has a plan; you must wait and see what it is." After looking back, I think you'll agree, he was right.

Ecclesiastes 3 says, "There is a time for everything." It also says there is a time to grieve, followed by a time to dance.

The Vietnam War has been over for more than 25 years, now, and for many, there still isn't a time for dancing. Many physically and emotionally damaged vets are not dancing yet. Many who lost loved ones in a seemingly senseless war are not yet dancing. There are those who will not see dancing on this earth, but there will come a time when millions will.

God speaks of a time when all wars, spiritual and physical, will be over. He describes peace this way through John in Revelation 21:3, "I heard a loud shout from the throne saying, 'Look, the home of God is now among men, and He will live with them and they will be His people. Yes, God, Himself, will be among them. He will wipe away all tears from their eyes, and there will be no more death, no sorrow, no crying, no pain—gone forever.'" In reading this, I think about Vietnam with all of its horrors. There were many tears, much pain and death, and grievous sorrow. But it is only temporary. Someday, all of the negatives of that war will not even be remembered.

When that time comes, I will join many grateful ones, because the time will finally have arrived when war will be over, forever.

The time for dancing will be just beginning—a time that will never end.

Chapter Nineteen

Art from Heaven

will never make another piece of jewelry!" I spoke these words
and left the jewelry class at USC for the last time, in 1965. I was
glad to be done, working in detail with metal. Now, 35 years later,
I have made not just one piece of jewelry but millions of pieces.
Never say, "Never."

I make jewelry items today out of gold, silver, and pewter.
Among the pewter items we have created, Christians' sayings re-
sembling popular retail item logos catch the attention of interested eyes. More specifically, we have created bottle caps with
truism sayings of the Christian. For example, while in Atlanta,
attending the Christian Booksellers Convention Show, I showed
the "bottle caps" that resemble Coke® signs. They were a real hit.
I never realized that the real Coke® headquarters was in that very
city, Atlanta. My wife, Polly, handed out 500 of these caps to book-
store owners to wear on their convention entry badges. The Coke®
look-alike had its competition, though. I have included a display
page of some of the bottle caps produced.

One of the renderings I painted for this book was taken from
an actual photo in Vietnam, after one of ours had just finished an
intense battle. The man in the foreground is drinking his Coke®,
while the soldier in the background was preparing his appetite for

Gatorade®. My bottle cap is appropriately titled "Jesus Is Greater Aid." Among the "God-wiser" cap, "God Is Cool" cap, "John 3:16" ticket, "Jesus" milk carton, and the "Hell, the real fry" bag all bring back the Vietnam moments of memory and needs. We needed soothing drinks, were hungry for fries that weren't there (except for the hot jungles), and longed for the fresh milk to camouflage our military ration-prescribed meals.

The most unusual of all the items made is the Jesus nut. This is not as it seems—a flippant description of an enthusiast for Christ but more, far more than that. The Jesus nut is about the only thing that stuck in my mind from helicopter mechanical school. This nut is the very core (center) of the helicopter that is essential to keeping the helicopter together. Unbelievably, the military and mechanics commonly term this item the, "Jesus Nut." What could be more central to this story than the Jesus Nut, me? After all, Jesus did hold me together as I flew in all the choppers in Vietnam.

Even though God's gospel is anything but peanuts, the thread of His message is held in a nutshell from the Bible passage, John 3:16. And the believers and many non-believers, alike, want their own admittance ticket to heaven. I wanted to share the secret that Jesus is their *only* ticket in.

As for Russia, they needed a smiling face after years of oppression from faith. So I capped off my message to them in Russian letters saying "Jesus loves you."

My remark at USC came from my art preference, which was painting and drawing, as they have always been. These were my loves; even at five years old I could hardly wait to grab my crayons and give a piece of paper a real workout.

My first real combat was in art, when I attempted to draw pirates on sinking ships. It was great fun and exciting. I would accompany the scene with special home-made noises while acting out the battles on paper.

More than 50 years later, I am emerged in the very same thing, but without the noises. Oils and canvas are now the heart of my rendering while I capture the intensity of the Vietnam war, much as I did more than 30 years ago in Vietnam.

Now, I paint to illustrate this book. Although my paint brushes and oils were left idle for years, it took only a couple of paintings to brush through canvases, one a week. Because of the Vietnam War, I hope to display in a one-man show at the Veterans Center. Because of the war, I look forward to creating some bronze sculptures—never before attempted. Because of the war, I am enjoying art with much anticipation, as never before, and with other art challenges. I literally go to war on canvas and with jewelry. My jewelry war is reaching far away countries: Russia, Germany, etc., "bombing" inside these nations with Gospel "bombs"—powerful, explosive "bombs" hitting the masses. Souls are being blown from the kingdom of darkness to the Kingdom of light—souls once almost obliterated by Communism.

Small bottle caps with Scriptures written in Russian are the latest ammunition the Lord has provided—on pewter with Russian letters that look like Pepsi Cola® proclaiming, "Jesus loves you." Calvary Chapel "troops" of Christian soldiers drop these "bombs." One Russian who saw these caps asked what it was, and got saved. He's known, now, as the Billy Graham of Russia. Perhaps the bottle cap explosion will mushroom out all over Russia, much like the bomb dropped in New Mexico, but to build lives, not destroy them.

Chapter Twenty

Now—Seeing
the Past

T hirty years after Vietnam, the memories still linger. None of
these years have been dull. Life has held many adventures and
surprises around every corner.

Attending USC once more, right after Vietnam, I received a
Master of Fine Arts degree. And again, I re-aimed my target for
teaching, once more in Orange County. This time, Huntington Beach
became my war ground for educating, at Fountain Valley High
School.

The students of Fountain Valley were the highlight of my 10-
year teaching career. Another victory was won. As in Villa Park
High School, there was a variety of characters: the hippies, straights,
jocks, druggies, and surfers. I must not forget the beauties, and
Fountain Valley had its share. Like my grandfather who was a beauty
contest judge in England, I mentally judged the merits of the beauties of the high school. Unlike my grandfather, however, who married his 17-year-old winner of the contest, I merely stood on the
sidelines and appreciated.

Incidentally, my classes had many 17-year-old winners. One
was Sheri Roberts, a cheerleader and a knockout. Her face ended
up on a billboard on the Coast Highway in California. The picture
showed her holding a soft drink. Another beauty was a fifteen year

old named Michelle, with blue eyes that came right out of heaven. She was gorgeous, and on occasion would stroll through my art bungalow during lunch time. I will never forget her face, knowing with certainty that she was destined for something big. It would be impossible for her to go unnoticed; I was right. She became homecoming queen three years later and Miss Orange County from there.

Eight years later, I saw Michelle's name on the subtitle of a movie showing on television. I called my roommate, Paul, to see if he remembered that she had attended our high school. He said, "No, I don't."

I prodded, "Don't you remember the gorgeous teeny bopper, surfer girl named Michelle Pfeifer? Surely you would remember her if you were there at that time."

After seeing Grease II on TV, we watched the rest of her movies as she progressed through great acting skills—with her beauty—to the heights of stardom. It is hard to imagine from the time of her teenage days that she would ever go that far. She seemed so quiet and introspective, but many things were stirring in her head, as I later discovered.

My roommate, Paul, would have noticed Michelle if he had been there then. Paul, himself, was continually being swooned over by the girls, who tried to catch a glimpse of him through the windows of their classrooms. He was 6'2", a blond surfer, with a face like Leonardo De Caprio, with an Olson surname. To the girls, he was like a Norwegian god. He knew the girls were eyeing him, but didn't give them the time of day (with the exception of one named Lisa.)

I wondered why Paul didn't seem to care much, but soon I was to learn that he wasn't a happy person. He said, "I want what you've got."

I asked, "What's that?"

"I want God in my life," he answered

I prayed for him, then, and at first I thought he got a little too much of Him.

The next day, Paul was on the surfer hill, a campus hangout where only surfers dared to trod. He was at the hilltop with a spellbound audience of surfer (peers), listening to him preach like John the Baptist, listening intently. To Paul, God was *very* real, and 30 years later, today, he continues to be just as real. Paul married my pastor's daughter and lives in Colorado Springs with his wife and four daughters.

There was another teenager nicknamed Jack (J.C. in school circles). Jack was the true definition of a surfer with a broad smile. He attracted all the ladies at the high school and became a mentor to each one in the art of kissing. Besides kissing, he also was a jewelry artist with so much refinement in the craft that even I learned a few things from him. This guy persuaded me into making jewelry for the local Christian book store. In the meantime, I shared Christian truths with him. One of his claims to fame was that he was Alice Cooper's cousin—a real look-alike. This, however, held no truth, whatsoever, no relationship at all.

Jack's kissing continued throughout high school—a Casanova with the coeds. As his skill become more adept, he really built up a reputation with his classmates.

The funny thing is, is that only yesterday, while finishing this book, I met the real Alice Cooper who was sitting behind me in the next pew with his beautiful wife at his side at a Baptist Church. The real Cooper does have the very same features of Jack; however, the real Cooper believes in Jesus Christ, now—one of the fellowship of Christians. Hallelujah!

There was one more student I shouldn't leave out; her name was Karen Roderick. Karen didn't smile. Instead, she always frowned. One day she told me she was an atheist. She didn't keep her indented countenance, but broadened her face into a smile the day Paul and I loaded her in my 1971 Dodge van that was packed with high school kids and headed to a Calvary Chapel tent to hear a 20-year-old preacher, Greg Laurie, tell us about God.

After the message, Karen looked at me with a smile I had never seen before and said, "Thanks for taking me here. Now, I know God." The smile never faded from then on. Shortly after, however, she had the opportunity to smile right into the face of the One she had met that night in the tent. Karen left our planet after being killed in a motorcycle accident. At the graveside, her mom broke a smile and said to me, "Thanks for telling little Karen about God." Today, when I pass the Good Shepherd Cemetery, I look over at the site where Karen is buried and think, *Someday, I will see her again and, when I do, she will still be smiling.*

Chapter Twenty-One

The '60s and '70s

ook at all the lonely people; where do they all come from . . . "
sang the Beatles in the 1960s. One day, I agreed with them, as I
saw almost everyone I knew trying to get un-lonely through the
isms, asms and spasms. I saw so much loneliness that it became
the prime subject of my artwork. Even as early as 1963, I painted
the lonely—a picture called "Bus Street," which became my first,
major art award.

Was loneliness from the void of belief, or void in trust in the
government? Teenagers needed questions answered then. These
Vietnam War years were iffy years. People needed stability in those
uncertain days. In the meantime, I needed to make a living and
wanted to teach.

Numerous times I repeated the same question, "Are there any
teaching positions available?" Finally, one response came back with
a, "No; I'm sorry—only in art." I responded, "That's exactly what I
want!" The person said, "Well, you couldn't have called at a better
time, because we just got word that one of the art teachers quit. Do
you have an application on file?" I said, "No." "Could you be here
in an hour for an interview?" I said, "Yes!"

The whole event had taken me by such surprise that I sat in
my green Chevy in silence for several minutes. The job was mine!

I was a teacher once again. While the students were engrossed in their art projects, they raised all sorts of questions. "Hey, Mr. Bowen, do you believe in evolution? My science teacher told me it is fact. What do you think?" How could I legally respond to that?

Since many of the students had brothers in Vietnam, I showed them my slides of Vietnam. Then more questions would crop up about brothers, uncles, cousins, and classmates of theirs who were killed in various causes. Three from my class, alone, were killed in auto accidents, and another was electrocuted. Kids wanted to know what was beyond the grave. Another very popular football player was murdered at a mini-market one night. This prompted even more questions. Then one student questioned, "Mr. Bowen, where was God when that guy was shot and stabbed to death?" There were all these deaths, and Karen too.

After a series of questions, I had a talk with God. I said, "What should I do the next time a kid asks me my opinion about God? Should I ignore him or her?"

Suddenly, there was very big news on campus. The vice principal was in a terrible head-on collision, which took his and his wife's life. You can imagine how this heart-breaking news hit us all!

At this point, I asked a science professor, "What are you teaching about life and the beyond?" He very bluntly replied, "I don't believe in the evolutionary theory. I don't have the faith to believe it." He then added: "Many scientists in the know on this subject have bailed on the Darwin view." He told me they were jumping off the Darwin propaganda wagon in droves. He said, "Somehow, the facts have not filtered down into the lower echelons of learning. I instruct this subject to the kids in my science class because my own kids need food in their mouths."

So went the 1970s. During those years I spent most of my time with other people's kids, because I had none of my own. That bothered me, so I asked God about it. There seemed to be no answer. Rather than get all bugged about it, I buried myself in crafting jewelry, mainly wedding rings with Christian symbols. This type of art was a craft, at first, learned in the midst of teaching it to high school students. The next thing I knew, jewelry became a business that took off all over the country, landing in Bible stores all across America.

It was greatly rewarding to create things people liked, even to make money doing it. School kids were apprenticing in my business until the business grew so much that I had to stop teaching just to handle it.

During this episode, I continued to keep my eyes open for the lady of my dreams. False alarms crossed my path and then Vicki Flower appeared. Spotting her, I was certain that God made her just for me. I was so convinced, I told her so and downstream found out what love was *not* all about. Later on, she married a pastor.

Learning about Vicki's marriage to a pastor, contrasted to your knowledge of me, now, you are probably wondering about my ever going down the aisle. At that time, so did I wonder. But when I turned 39, something different happened.

I met the cutest seven-year-old girl with big, beautiful blue eyes staring at me through a thick head of blond hair. This seven year old was the daughter of a single mom at that time. When I told my four roommates that I believed I had met my daughter, they thought I was kidding. Three months later, however, when I brought her mom home for a visit, I am sure all of them wondered if she had any single look-alike sisters.

I was right about the mom. The little girl, Kelley, with eyes that seemed to ask me, "Will you come home with me and be my dad?" drew me to her wonderful mom, Polly, who soon became my wife.

When I met Polly, she was cleaning and taking care of households. She had recently run from a lifestyle in Hollywood where she was modeling, film making, and experiencing other aspects of that world that left her empty and searching. Polly, like Paul and Karen, had come to know God, and a new life for her had begun.

We had a storybook wedding under a huge oak tree in her parents' back yard in South Pasadena, California. As Polly and I started our adventures together, we soon added to our threesome with a new daughter—a sister for Kelley who was 10 then. Suzie became another joy for us. But the road Polly and I traveled was rocky, as there were business and health problems that came in cycles. Just when things were looking up, my idyllic bubble popped once again.

....

Chapter Twenty-Two

Surfing the Coaster

This roller coaster ride took me to a new low. I received another "Dear John" letter, only this time it was not mailed to me but was served to me. The letter didn't have stamps, but it did have an official government insignia at its top. Another Government letter that was not welcomed was about to jab me. Much like my Government letter with a bottom line stating I was to be drafted, this letter also had its bottom line with dated material. I was being served divorce papers, in other words, un-drafted. As usual, the unexpected roller coaster dive was deep, and I don't believe it is over yet. Knowing my Lord and God, the way I do, the ride on this coaster will soon be reaching the heights once more with God's guidance. With the Lord, you can't escape the thrills of His ride.

Today, I live with the same little 7 year old I met more than 17 years ago. At 24, she is married to Aaron, and they have just made me a first-time grandfather of Max Isaiah, during this writing on February 20, 2000. Suzie is now 14. We all live at the base of Mt. San Bernardino, nicknamed Miracle Mountain, by a "friend" I greatly admire.

My friend is Henrietta Mears—a wonderful prayer warrior. Here is a quote of one of her admirers:

Dr. Henrietta C. Mears has had remarkable influence, both directly and indirectly on my life. In fact, I doubt if any woman other than my wife and mother has had such a marked influence. Her gracious spirit, her devotional life, her steadfastness for the simple gospel and her knowledge of the Bible have been a continual inspiration and amazement to me. She is certainly one of the greatest Christians I have ever known!
—Dr. Billy Graham
(printed by the Billy Graham
Evangelistic Association)

Since Henrietta prayed for my mother, sister, and me, my life has gone through twists and turns—through the roller coaster rides in college, Vietnam, back to college, teaching high school again, to making jewelry and then to the foot of Miracle Mountain, where Henrietta's prayers first took place. God's will was working as she unleashed His will in prayer, waiting for His answers.

We had come full circle—God, Henrietta, the mountain, and me. Henrietta fell asleep one night, a few weeks after praying with my mother, in December 1962. Her sleep was eternal. None of this was by chance. The clincher was that my daughter, Kelley, met her husband, Aaron, at Forest Home, a Christian Center Henrietta started. What's in a name? Nothing. What in God's purpose? Everything.

Combating from Artist to Teacher

What about the Watts riots? At the time of the riots, I was stationed at "Fort USC," right where the riots raged. I made a night escape through the Figueroa exit onto the Harbor Freeway in Los Angeles, where bullets were picking off escapees. After my Vietnam tour, I returned to this same war zone to teach at Fremont High School, an uneasy location for a white to be roaming at night.

My first day of teaching, I had been warned of the school's location in the combat zone. Sure enough, my first day teaching was accompanied by incoming rockets—beer bottles. The hit was direct—direct to the head discipline principal—while training me

142

how to handle the unruly. Minutes later I found myself standing alone in the midst of 50 black warriors.

Guess who won? Actually, God did. He won them over by the love I showed them. They all knew I cared about them. The three biggest and toughest ones joined me on a backpacking trip, and word got around that I was okay. In fact, when a bunch of invaders attacked the campus, causing major injuries, I hid in a closet with these three guards protecting it.

Another touching experience took place in the classroom, when the football coach entered, all teary-eyed, and joined by an illiterate athlete. The coach begged me to change his grade so that his student could make it in the only thing he excelled—in sports. So, I did it. At the time, it seemed like the right thing to do.

Chapter Twenty-Three

Where Have All the People Gone?

My buddies were really characters, those whom I have known my entire life, school and military acquaintances, relatives, and some unexpected friends along the way. As I look back on all these special people, I find many interesting sorts with all kinds of paths they took.

Those whom I call my buddies, the ones I grew up with have all turned out successful. Lane Cash, my partner in investment with the go-cart, is now working for the State of California as a Probation Officer.

Mike Napier, who helped me rescue the heap of a go-cart from disaster to the grave, became an attorney in Arizona and was seen on a national news broadcast discussing youth problems.

Dennis, the Mole, has been teaching school at Tustin High School in Orange County, California, since 1971.

Another friend from high school, Ken Rheberg, often joined me in skipping summer school English in order to go surfing. Later he graduated the top of his class from Biola University. He is involved in writing a detailed and much researched story about the Kennedy assassination. The story shares new insights based on personal experience. I'm looking forward to its soon release.

Ron Shaffer, my college roommate, childhood friend, and correspondent during my Vietnam experience ended up in Vietnam, himself, writing for the *Stars and Stripes* newspaper. Now, he is a top journalist at *The Washington Post*. Ron produced a book on uncovering theft cover-up activities named, *Surprise, Surprise!*

Bob Myers, the matchmaker, also had a stint in Vietnam. He was one of my fraternity brothers who is now pursuing a law degree. He was also one of my Vietnam corresponding buddies.

Maxine, the Post Commander's wife is engrossed in an art colony in Arizona. When discharged from the military I sent her the Christian book, The *Late Great Planet Earth*, which she loved.

Two of the platoon sergeants from Basic Training reappeared in my life. Both of these men loved bellowing orders and got big kicks out of being served. I ran into one of these sergeants who I found in roll reversal if I ever saw one. Several years after my Army tour at McDonalds in Stockton, California, it was just like old times. This time, I gave the orders and he did the serving—I would never have expected this!

The other platoon sergeant came face-to-face with me in Arizona, somewhere. I was gassing up at a Chevron Gas Station, and it seemed just like old times. His uniform vaguely resembled the military chevrons, only in reverse. I was greeted with a warm smile, until I became recognized. Then, the order was given, and serving began. I ordered him to fill the gas tank, check the oil, and check the windshield wipers, and he filled, checked, and checked. I thought maybe we could joke around a bit, but the joke bombed, he got his target, and concentrated on the only tank he knew, now. Off I went, into the wild blue yonder, able to finally laugh—but still not in his presence.

My USC scholar associates have turned into success stories in their own endeavors. Looking at 1962 Marks Hall Dorm picture reminds me of each person's personal victories. Earl, for one, became a dentist in Brea, California.

Dennis Boucher was one of my fraternity brothers, shown pictured with me. The fraternity house shared many events inside and outside its walls. Certain instances stand out, like the budding Beach Boys practicing outside on Frat Row, and David Nelson shared about Ricky, his brother, and their Kappa Sigma experiences at USC.

Then, Louie Zamborini spoke at the house, telling us about his world record in the mile run, and his 1936 Olympics experience of climbing the flag pole and lowering the Nazi flag—a move Hitler didn't forget. Louie also shared his World War II survival story, which culminated into another world record—the longest recorded survival at sea without food or water—nearly 20 days, if I recall correctly.

My frat friend, Ron Rousse, asked me to go with a group, one night, to a USC Friday night basketball game. Plans changed for me that night, and I ended up with my date, Sheri Clayton, who was to receive a beauty award instead. Had I been with Ron and the group, I might have been hit by a hit-and-run drunk who headed his vehicle right into the crowd crossing the street. Unfortunately, Ron was killed that night when hit and tossed 50 yards. And we wonder why plans change. Ron was a well-respected person and too young to die, just as those who died in Vietnam, who had hopeful futures. This is all so unfair, but only God knows. The comforting factor is that Ron had his eyes on God when I knew him.

Another man who left a standing impression was a visitor in one of my USC graduate classes. This man, whom I didn't know at the time, became my father-in-law. That was 35 years ago.

The Nam war years had some other outstanding figures who became famous for their various impressions on society. Each was radical and influential in his own passions, but became diametrically radical in opposite directions from his onset. Jerry Rubin, Bob Dylan, and Jane Fonda all became radical for Jesus, once they had convinced themselves of another way to live.

Specifically, Jerry Rubin told us to kill our parents; later, he told us to love them. Bob Dylan sang and played his message of ". . . the answers are blowing in the wind . . . ." Later, he found the answers from the One who blows the wind. Jane Fonda expounded on resisting fighting the Viet Cong, fighting the Establishment all the way, and now is fighting for Jesus in her own way—the only One who could rescue the lost of Viet Cong and our own lost Government.

This proves that radicals are not always bad, necessarily—being one myself, but the radical can turn radically good. Even God,

Himself, is radical—radically perfect and good—in saving those who are radical in their own way.

After the Dear John letter from Ginger, I lost touch. But before she became missing we attended a Billy Graham Crusade together and she did not miss her calling, but went forward to receive Christ in salvation.

My parents, much older now, are both very active. Mom golfs regularly and boasts of the holes in one among her achievements. Although she is not the club champion, she is standing next to Arnold Palmer in one of her pictures, which makes you think she is a champion. Women's Bible Study is another of her activities, as well as trying to make people happy, including my dad. She shines in these events of giving.

Dad gives, too, by carefully tending his beautiful garden of rose bushes and orange trees (almost two trees, since my dog, Sara got to the root of one tree). This time, her bite was worse than her bark! And, don't let me forget the strawberries Dad nourishes. When he goes north to Canada, I take over these responsibilities for six months during his absence when he sneaks into Gibson Landing in British Columbia. There, he continues his love of gardening while protecting his community garden space from his 92-year-old neighbor gardener.

Chapter Twenty-Four

THE GUYS—Our Gang

Riverside in the '50s and '60s were full of orange groves where we all played—our favorite hang-out. It was our habit to wear football helmets to protect us from the rotten orange fights we had in the groves. I distinctly remember getting a hit directly in the ear—rotten orange, juice, pulp, and all. My ear was never so juicy and it took forever to get it all out.

Bonnie Weatherwax was my first girlfriend in Fifth Grade. Mike Napier took her away from me shortly after, when he stared singing "My Bonnie lies over the ocean..." So much for the Bonnies in my life. Between Bonnie and high school, Mike courted many a lass, but then there was Joan Gibbs—Lorretta Young look-alike, with crystal blue-green eyes. Mike lent her to me to capture in pastels for history's sake.

The Bully and the "Fonz"

I chose the quick route, instead of the mile, coming home from school one day. Off I went riding my bike into the grove that bordered my property. All of a sudden I found myself dumped on the ground by the neighborhood bully with a patch over one eye. He was huge compared to my slight frame and his good eye bore the expression of a short distance between me and him. With confidence in distance, and riled by the last event, I snapped back with the worst words I could muster. The margin wasn't enough, however, and I was pursued again. I couldn't peddle hard enough and, again, found myself on the dirt. Looking like one of the rotten oranges fallen from the tree I resumed my travel home. Mike Napier spotted the sight that I was and decided to plan revenge. He got his older brother Dan, the "Fonz", to get his ruffian group together for the day of revenge. Soon after, we never saw the bully any more in the grove. Unfortunately, the Fonz and gang had more victories to win and I became their next target.

The afternoon was quiet enough and I was getting some play time out front. The Fonz decided he and his buddies were bored. The next thing I knew, I was scrambling down the street as fast as I could and then downed by the Fonz and his friends. What was I to do, now? There, up in the tree, were my pants dangling from the branches—good entertainment for the neighbors. How could I get home in this condition and not be embarrassed when passing by Bonnie Weatherwax's house? I never climbed a tree so quickly in all my life, snatched my pants, and proceeded on my way. It started out to be a nice afternoon! Mike Napier continues to remind me of the predicament, so I'll never forget.

Personalities

Dave Adler—When Doug Sterret and Alan Settle were left in the dust of Santa Barbara, and I moved to Riverside, Dave Adler became my "best bud", when I was six. I was shot dead while roaming the orange groves by "Hop-a-long Cassidy" Dave. I plummeted to the ground, a goner, then got up to meet my new buddy, Dave. After cowboys, we became anglers at the fishing holes with our dads. I'm sure we didn't miss a fishing hole in Riverside, then. This is the same Dave whose fence I massacred with arrows. His dog, incidently, took all the free arrows on his side of the fence and marched proudly with the finds into the orange grove to break them in half, each one.

Ron Schaffer—Ron was the Mark Twain and CEO of our bunch. What a storyteller he was, keeping us all entertained with his verbalizing. He was never at loss for words and his verbal use of the English language was unique in descriptions. Sometimes his acting was almost as good as his storytelling. In college, he became a sports writer for the Riverside Press, then wrote for the Stars and Stripes while in Vietnam, and finally writes for the Washington Post. One result of Ron's writing led Coach Tarkanian, the Riverside City College Basketball Coach, on to coaching professional basketball. All of us who went to Vietnam received special letters from Ron, as well as Ron who served his turn as well.

Among the letters Ron wrote me, I'll share his experience as guest at a Vietnamese dinner table.

I've been to dinner at student's houses four times the first week of this month. The class I have now is far the best I've had. Very bright, and we're very close. Their homes are at poverty level by our standards—cardboard and tin roofs - but the hospitality, the sincerity, is overwhelming. The mother and sisters worked hard in the kitchen, coming out only to serve one course after another. As was the case in three of the four homes, the source of heat for cooking was not gas or electricity, but wood. The food was way over their heads, price-wise. The wild variety of some of the food was way over my head also.

At one of the homes, the first course brought on was eggs in the shell—duck eggs. The other American instructor remarked that hard-boiled duck eggs were very similar to chicken eggs, only the yolk was larger and more orange. I was resolved to eat the duck eggs without much thought. We did begin talking, however, about one of the delicacies of Vietnam that we had heard about, but had never seen, This incredible dish is simply a chick or duck egg 15-17 days developed in the 21-day cycle. The embryo, complete with eyes, beak, bones, claws, and feathers, is eaten right along with the blood veins-laced yolk and other oils.

Well then, Luong and the other students passed around their duck eggs. I said a silent prayer of thanks that I would never have to eat this special delicacy. Then I took a spoon and cracked the "hard-boiled egg." A green oil ran out. In the middle of this oil was a clump of feathers. I looked at the other American instructor and he looked at me. "You guessed it," he said.

By now, the half-dozen Vietnamese students were sucking in their eggs. Of course, as is their custom, the dinner guest is expected to eat everything served him or the host. And particularly, the mother of the host, is deeply insulted. Well, I ate squid and octopus and raw seaweed and raw fish, and thought I could tackle anything, but when I saw students inhaling a mouthful of slimy feathers and bones, I almost created a mess of my own right there on the table.

I could not bring myself to eat the thing. So I played with it, cracking the shell, moving the body around in the bowl, taking frequent sips of beer and keeping my mouth busy with lots of bread. I could see a slight pained expression on the mother when she hauled away my still-full egg bowl. She must have seen great relief on my face.

Next came the curry, a kind of stew, or catchall for bizarre meats. A little disgusted with myself for not eating the delicacy, I decided to really dig into the curry. My first mouthful tasted like barf smells. I asked what it was, and the host said, "Oh, pig stomach and intestines." I didn't eat any more curry.

They passed the peppers, the elongated, red ones that the Mexican eat. I knew they were extremely hot. But everyone was watching me and egging me to eat one, and to demonstrate to all my bravery (and to get rid of the barf taste) I popped in a whole pepper. At first, nothing happened and I was proud. Then the fires of hell grabbed my tongue. The stinger of a bee was injected deep into every tiny taste bud. Tears came quickly. My esophagus closed. I had much trouble breathing, Liquid didn't help, mor was there much comfort in the guffawing all around. This condition lasted for five minutes and lessened to mere agony. This was as good a condition as any, I suppose, to try the next course. It was some kind of soup with stuff floating in it.

It looked like cabbage. About a quarter of an inch thick, nearly transparent, with light veins and bubbles inside. It was jelly-like in substance. Even though I hate cabbage, I was hoping it was cabbage. "Cabbage?", I inquired hopefully. "No,"

Luong answered. "Cooked pig skin." I quickly spotted the bread tray again. Bread is big at Vietnamese dinners.

The last delicacy had been brought on in my honor. It was one of the most popular dishes of the county. Cooked chicken head. Luong started at the neck, ripping away the outer skin and chomping on tendons, clearing to the bone. Then a chomp into the top of head to savor the brain. Everything was eaten except the beak.

After the ordeal, our talk drifted to an ancient dish of the Chinese. Kings of China used to serve to their European guests a live monkey per man. Then around came a small mallet. Guests were instructed to crack the monkey on the skull and then dig in. This is still, done to a limited extent in Vietnam today. "Not many do it," Luong said. "The monkey is too expensive.

Yes...East is East and West is West, and Kipling certainly must have been thinking about dinners when he wrote that.

Mike Napier—He was the athlete of our group—a true body surfer. Besides being a great baseball player, and a man for the ladies, he also was a speed demon. At a weak moment, I mentioned to his father that he was a peddle-to-the-metal guy and he soon was walking. Sorry Mike.

Lane Cash—Lane was my partner in crime and creativity with the go-cart. We also shot together, archery that is. The go-cart and archery are lasting memories. Looking out for one another in our group was always a must. One day we heard that Lane's father had a heart attack. It was in the moment of bravery he fell to his death. Lane's father was pursuing a thief and trying to catch the guy when his heart gave out. We all felt deeply for Lane.

Dennis Boucher—He lived in a mansion on a bluff. I can remember many times fishing and hunting with our bows and arrows for some innocent prey. We got into more adventures than can be described here, so I've included some of them in other parts of this book.

Ken Rheberg—Dobbie Gillis, where are you? My fourteen-year-old Suzie pointed him out—the handsome one. What about me, Suzie? I guess Suzie didn't consider me the "fairest" of them all. Ken won the title and even played Dobbie Gillis' part in the Poly High School play. All the girls thought he was it!

These all were my buddies—the gang. Our gang was not the same as a gang known today. We were just a bunch of guys who lived in the same neighborhood, seeking youthful fun. Today, the gangs have leaders with goals of destruction. Our gang used baseball bats to split ball seams, while the gangs today use them for splitting heads. We used water balloons to get people's attention; the gangs today use assault rifles. We played hide and seek, but the gangs today seek and kill. We used to shoot marbles; the gangs today shoot drugs. Our gang rode bikes at night while smelling the orange blossoms of Riverside. Today, the blossom trees have funny names on them and are stuck in cement. We drove cars to show off to the girls, the gangs today drive cars to disturb and kill. We looked for girls and fun from our cars; the gangs today look for expressions on people faces to incite a fight and kill. Our Riverside is still great, but definitely not the same Riverside of the '50s and '60s. The Riverside of yore is gone forever, now, never to return. We still have our memories, though. There were nights of camping out in the back yard after our moms' feasts. We would lie under the stars, smelling the orange blossoms, telling stories, joking, and then tried to fall asleep. At dawn, we would wake up to catch the "big" one in a local pond.

School in our days was a place to learn the three Rs; today they zone out beyond the Zs. We painted murals in school, then; the murals of today is graffiti. Life has changed for the worse. I'm glad I lived in the earlier days when life was simple fun and life was comfortable—a safer, more productive day.

Letter from the Gang

All of us received draft notices in this era of the Nam war. We all kept in touch, not matter where we landed. Life, itself, became a familiar thread in all our letters. One (of anonymous nature due to privacy) stands out among them. After writing, a tome of words, I received a response that left many questions unanswered. Now, 30 years later, I want the opportunity to respond to questions in his letter:

> Edda, I read your 30-page book several times, very carefully. There are so many deep thoughts I can only adequately respond when I see you. Really admire your convictions, Edda. You would be disappointed in me, though. Because if religion is the active worship of a superior being, I guess I have no religion. I do, however, have strong feelings toward a humanitarian ethic.
>
> I deny no man his religion and respect any man who sincerely worships his god. Nothing, to me is more ludicrous than the centuries of religious persecution and intolerance, and torture, and suffering, and discrimination, and misunderstanding over religion. If a man thinks his god is a turtle egg, I respect his belief, as much as the most devout Buddhist or Christian (if that religion is based on similar values.)
>
> Have seen much of the work and devotion applied to Buddhism here, in the Orient. Who is to say who is right, not I. I merely observe and take spiritual comfort in my humanitarian ethic.

My own response to my friend is:

> If I were to agree with my friend that Jesus is a dead man and teacher, then all that is left is a temporary, futile humanitarian ethic, at best, which ends, finally, in the grave. How hopeless! But if Jesus is alive, then what Jesus had to say throws humanitarian ethic to the wind, along with every other god from the turtle egg to the mighty dollar into the eternal garbage can of cosmic emptiness. What would be the purpose that He would ever roam the earth and have a non-com-

promising book established of His life - a book that has never changed in thousands of years? Wow! Thank God Jesus is alive. He is the only hope that we have.

Proof, one may say is the missing link. There is proof, however, found in the Bible's book of John. It contains all the proof needed for anyone. Reading the book of John will convince any reader, if read in its entirety. If more proof is needed, then there is a book titled "The Case for Christ" or another book titled "Evidence that Demands a Verdict". Proof is found through these writings which lead to the edge of a barrier between you and God, Himself. The barrier is only crossed as one takes the step of faith. When the first step is taken by saying a **sincere** "Yes!" to Jesus, troublesome questions will disappear. God will toss them to the wind. This is very much a personal trip in belief. Only sincerity will be the guide to the real answers. Try it, just try it with the realness of your being and see what happens! My own life has been so enriched through taking that step. I can't share anything more precious than this, the real meaning of hope.

Memories

The Man's Meal

A man's dinner already eaten, the bet was on. The five of us discussed the outlandish bet of an eight-minute "scarf". Who was to take the bet? What was the bet? Ron, the master of design, challenged to treat any one of us who could eat two Bob's Big Boy double deckers, French fries, a bowl of chili, and a chocolate malt on top of the already devoured meal in eight minutes. There was silence, the wheels turned and finally a taker was at hand. Dennis, the "Mole" was our quinea pig—a pig's meal, all right. The challenge was on, the audience was ready for entertainment, and the clock began ticking. Mind you, this was a heavy bet on a full stomach. The ending clause mentioned that the culprit couldn't barf. This got a lot of attention by now, and even the waitresses were in on it.

The first bite, second, third, the hamburger was gone. The second one was at hand, down it went. Here came the chili, followed by the fries, and the coupe de gras was the cold malt, to the rescue, that froze the esophagus from further action. Seven seconds remained and the bet was won, so far. The second "Man's Meal" was gone, finished. We wondered, however, if it was to appear again. No, not yet. The "sampler" arose, slowly, carefully, and crept toward the rest room ahead. The "whale" kept his target of the room. When was Jonah to appear? The clock had stopped, but his stomach hadn't, yet. His body was in turmoil from the treat. The treat was soon to die out when our experimenter turned inside out before reaching his destination. Good try, all lost, and there was a lot to pay.

J-Ball

There goes another one—crash. One window after another became the victim of our follies with baseballs. Even a glass table took the brunt of a toss. Whiffle balls became the "name of the game", now. We all were in this thing together. Before you knew it, "Our Gang" gathered for another whiffle affair—no matter where we were. We met in Washington, D.C., the beach, Riverside, San Diego, parks and any other place just to meet and play whiffle ball "J-Ball". Our whiffle ball widows got left in the dust to damn our darn socks—but no more broken glass. You see, our socks were holier than we were at that time.

Those were our J-Ball days, and will probably continue to play into our J-Ball older daze. Picture us in our ballooned shorts with toothpick legs, scurrying to meet the challenge of hitting the ball, seeing the ball, or even catching the ball. But which is it—the whiffle ball or a bald head? There's it goes; was it the ball or a toupee? There's Mole on the mound, Ron's striking at home plate (was it the guy or the back that went out?), Lane's lying at short stop with myopic Ron missing the target, Napier catching what he can see, Adler's out in left—propped up by the fence, and I'm trying to remember the score. Who's on first? Snap, crackle, pop! The crispier we get the louder the game. There goes the runner—down that is—because his knees buckle and his belt won't. Did anyone remember the score? Rheberg is missing in action. The game has taken on new dimensions; we're all older I guess.

The Car

One Saturday during high school, we escaped to the luring Laguna Beach surf. Napier and Cash came by to kidnap me from yard duties. They told me, "Get in." There was no room in the Metro Rambler. They continued, "Get in and we all were off!" A coin was tossed to determine who was to cramp up in the non-back seat. Only a pretzel could cram into this hole. I was the chosen one who got into the "Houdini" scrunch and was forgotten all the way to Laguna, while the radio blasted "Big Bopper" and Buddy Holly tunes. All my pleads for release were ignored. My remains were pried out of the "sardine can" at our destination. While they headed for the cliff of the surf, I tried my best to reassume normal posture. It was a fun day for Mike and Lane. We all got roasted, but the round trip agreement still stood. I was doomed for the "Sardine can" again, but now I was also a roasted crab. Reassembling in the back, once more, we headed home. Home at last, cramped and baked, I had to return to the push mower and thick grass as red as I was. Mike and Lane left laughing their heads off. Will I ever forgive them or the American Motor Company for creating the Rambler—even God who created the sun?

Drawing Straws

We had a common war zone—our apartment at USC. After one year, picture this: the walls were decorated with posters—stuck with bonding glue, the rugs were matted with leftovers of all sorts, the furniture took on its share of decor, too. The air, itself, became bombarded with flying Pepsi cola, water balloons, and other delicacies of prank. Who could sleep with another bombardment around the next minute? Who could have order in the place of chaos? Prank and re-prank left Dennis with his clothes flying in the breeze, then plunging to the first floor alley full of grease, after he opened the door which held his clothes on a fragile line—doomed to fall. The apartment was apart. The time for recognition was upon us. The call was made after drawing straws to plead for our deposit back. The brave one, Ron, dialed, spoke, then listened. The receiver took the brunt. We stood frozen, waiting for the message. We heard guttural explosions, silent screeches, and words not to be repeated. We didn't get our deposit refunded. Our punishment was the draft of Vietnam.

Chapter Twenty-Five

Sharing the Times

I had five reasons for letting you into this remarkable world and life we all share. The first, is to share. People's real experiences are so unique for each person, and communicating the specials is a way to take another on the trip I've experienced. Though many similarities exist in the lives of human beings, the differences are so greatly pronounced that the trip becomes a specialized tour. I want to include others in on the interesting twists and turns of what should be so normal, almost boring. Life doesn't allow for boring, though.

As an artist, I find stirring of emotions a gift, for some people, through expression: on canvas, in statues, in moldings, in jewelry, in writing, etc. (An aside: One of my gifts is to try to include the reader as a partner. In its many forms, art is the bridge for the reader and I to meet.)

Laughing is my second reason to share. Laughter heals and unites, a good exercise for us all. To take the eerie, serious, and terrible to find humor—any humor—slightly visible within these boundaries helps to keep one's perspective. Then adjustment makes reality become more remote, as if spying on the secret adventures of experience. Victory over ignorance, self-degradation, and the obvious is always the plus of life.

Battle is so familiar to us all. There's the battle of getting out of bed when you're tired, the battle of getting to a destination in a crowd, the battle of overcoming things in one's life, the battle of demeanor, the battle of communication, and the battle of war. We enter so many battles each day, without even being enlisted, drafted, or being aware.

My third reason is the enjoyment of telling a story. War is a topic that fascinates. My great grandfather told of his fighting in the Boer War, in South Africa, where he saw soldiers choking to death on their swollen tongues from lack of water. He was one of Queen Victoria's guards. She gave him an autographed chocolate box with her picture on it. I was so fascinated by his story, my great grandfather gave the box to me.

My parents distinctly remember my unique qualities. One specific instance was when they discovered I made the front page of the local Riverside paper for ROBBING A BANK. This truly happened, but it was legal. My mug shot was printed for all to see in the July 25, 1956 issue of the *Riverside Press Enterprise*.

Besides my parents, at seven years old, my daughter Kelley had a good belly laugh when I told her this story. Even today, Kelley laughs as I repeat it to my fourteen-year-old daughter, Suzie. Suzie doesn't find it so funny, but mumbles under her breath about funny old Dad. I guess 56 is old to a fourteen-year-old.

My grandmother told her own stories about her Welsh uncle who gave her a first-time visit. Due to the excitement of his visit, he wanted to take the fastest transport available, transport with low fare for the steerage passengers. He chose the Titanic. As later discovered, a meager few from that class made it. He was one who *did not*!

Grandfather Summerbell told of his own shirker assignment as the General's librarian during World War I. It was a good thing he, as I, wasn't on the front lines because of his own, unique love of life—even to the ants, etc., when they wage their own warfare into areas where they shouldn't be. If he had to go to Vietnam, he may not have wanted to spare the mosquitoes, however. The only fierce battle I had in Nam was with the mosquitoes, and that was intense! If the mosquito bayonets weren't in my hands, arms, or legs they were foolishly stuck in my paint while I yelled at them, "Kill, kill, kill!" as my staff sergeant had brainwashed me to yell.

Back to my grandfather, the *true* down-to-earth pacifist. With a "bayonet" needle, he stuck one of his pacifist dinner guests, accidentally. He had devised a contraption of pulleys, wires, and gears and hooked it up to the dining room table. When the perfect moment came, he pulled a lever attached to his chair, remote from the victim, and the wire released a needle into the chair's cushion. At will, he could reverse it—quite a prank! Imagine if he had not been a pacifist!

As previously mentioned, my dad had the best true stories. When in his 30s, he was so adept he even won awards through storytelling. As a radio actor, in Toronto, Canada he was a raconteur. His partner was a guy named Lorne Greene, who later showed up on television. Dad continued onto the stage and furthered his storytelling. As Santa Claus, with a flowing beard and plastic mask, he didn't go over too big with the moms and their frightened, crying children.

Dad likes to expound about his Warner experiences, where he worked while I was growing up. He worked, as he puts it, in the support area. His employer was the Warners Bra and Girdle Company. Now at 85, Dad, involves himself with Christian radio and television programs of the day, as well as his hobbies.

My fourth reason of sharing is wanting to feel important— honest an answer as it is. This stems from wanting to prove that there is real worth in those who have been put down by others. So, my motive is not to be prideful, but rather to heal, with the assurance that those who put others down have incorrect assessments and are the real losers. Being an underdog, so to speak, and learning from others that you can not do it at every turn of your life, eventually gave me the wherewithal to fight back and succeed.

I had the opportunity to read an article from the local Corona Del Mar paper about this guy who eventually attained success. It gave me a real boost of affirmation after reading it. At 25 years old, this anonymous guy wrote losing screen plays for 10 years, only because they were not finished in a timely way. He kept plugging on, however. One day, even after repeated rejection, he wrote about old guys in outer space. It just so happened that Clint Eastwood got a hold of it and is in the process of making a $100-million-budgeted movie—the "royalties" of not quitting. To this day, I am a non-quitter as has continued since I was young.

My friend Dennis Boucher (the Mole), was my major competition in art when I was in Second Grade. The Mole's artwork was so good that it ended up hung all over the school, in place of mine. Rather than be second, I decided to be first. I tried so hard to be first in art that I'm sure I never did what I was supposed to in other areas of learning. I did learn the ABCs, but reading them out loud made me sweat with embarrassment.

Finally, in junior high school, I heard a teacher direct a remark to me that changed my intellectual indifference. In a Southern drawl, my history teacher said, "Eddie, you just aren't college material!" That did it! That one remark made me think, *I'll show you!*

That one remark spurred me on to make honor roll in my Senior year of high school. I did not make the honor roll because I was smart, but because I was what my former concerned counselors called an achiever. I remembered what the counselors told my PTA President mom, explaining that an achiever is one who isn't smart but who has enough drive to make it look like he is. My mom was definitely not content with their explanation and to this day considers me a genius. These same counselors, who have now gone from this life, will now know the truth that before only God and I knew.

My senior grades got me into USC, where there were impossible obstacles. This is when I encountered the same English professor who gave me a mercy D and expressed his disapproval of my work in both looks and words. His combined summation of scrutinizing led me to believe that any writing I did would be doomed to fail.

Even though I was convinced that my writing was bad I said, "It doesn't have to be that way." Unbelievably, 30 years later, I pulled out my pencil and, after an almost 3-day binge, I wrote *Where Have All the Children Gone?*

What I never expected, happened. One Sunday morning, Dr. James Kennedy held up *Where Have All the Children Gone* on his

Christian television broadcast and said, "Read this book. It's well written and tells you the truth about abortion." Although the title, outline, cover, and certain content were left in tact, the credit mainly goes to D. A. Miller for the bulk of the writing.

At 15, I scored very low in a Boy Scout Archery Tournament in Palm Springs. When my buddies discouraged me by telling me I'd never be a Robin Hood shooter, I ignored them and determinedly decided to prove them wrong. Two years later, after making my next door neighbor's fence look like a machine gun target, I decided to take on the tournament challenge.

Ready to go for the challenge, my bow was not. Right in front of the Tournament bosses, I shot my first arrow as my bow broke in half. Not giving up, I continued to keep up the barrage on my neighbor's fence.

Finally, determined practice paid off, when I garnished a prize for marksmanship, and it was no joke. The news showed my winning mug shot and I retired the bow. Ten years later, I checked to see if my junior American Round Record of 656 out of a possible 804 was still holding. By that time, it wasn't. Some other Robin Hood robbed me of my title by then.

Chapter Twenty-Six

The Beauties

M y childhood friends and their beauties teased me because I was too scrawny. Mike Napier, who won the school prize beauty after running from one beauty to another, teased me all the time. Unlike muscular Mike with his persuasive demeanor, I was the opposite and was left out most of the time. However, I'll recount a couple of times I was on the inside.

Sandra Jennings, a 17-year-old beauty with a smile and face that left every high school guy in Riverside drooling, didn't seem to mind that I was less desirable. She used to take time to talk to me at the Mission Inn pool where her dad was coach. She actually gave me a lot of attention and liked talking to me. Only a few years later, she got the attention of the entire city, as well as me, as we sat glued to our television sets while she got "runner up" to Miss America. I still believe she had the prettiest face of any Miss America before or since then. She's in her late 50s, now, but I bet she still has that pretty face and smile.

I met Joy in a summer school English class. Her smile was as pretty as Sandra's—another beauty. Then, I was no longer tiny, but had grown to 6'2" and was in pretty good shape—still awkward, though. I asked her to attend a USC function, and she agreed. We only dated a couple of times. The next thing I knew, her picture was in the newspaper, showing her as Miss Riverside County. Today, Joy is a Riverside City Council Woman who continues to be beautiful.

A girl who graduated from the same high school as I did was the best beauty, however. From high school, she entered the Hollywood world of glitz. Her career toured her from modeling, to films, to a fast life certain to be connected to the rich and famous. None of the scene filled her void of an empty heart. She soon ran from the important lifestyle. Even the well-known Hollywood reporter, Leo Guild, couldn't capture her attention. When he asked her if he could write a book about her and call it *Polly and Me*—a second book in his series after his Heddy Lamar story *Ecstasy and Me*—she said, "No!" Polly's "No" stunned him; no one said, "No!" to Leo. All kinds of hopefuls were begging Leo for a story. But Leo wanted what Leo couldn't have—her beauty and intrigue. Polly didn't want that world.

One night, Polly sat across the dinner table from a playboy, named Hugh. For the longest time his mesmerizing stare tried to consume her, to entice her with a worldly "come hither" to fill the void.

Coincidentally, Polly had a void as well that didn't last long after that. The quick exodus from Hollywood and rescue by her concerned Aunt Eileen got her right on track at last. This track eventually led her to me and to our marriage in 1984.

Chapter Twenty-Seven

Plugging for Polly

Hesitating for quite some time, I thought about whether I should include a story about Polly's life with me. I decided it was a mistake to say nothing. Wanting to avoid any damage to either of us or our children, I will share about the most significant person of my later years, my wife and friend for 15 years.

I always have loved Polly and want to include the importance of her life in mine, even though Polly didn't think I loved her.

Sharing what Polly, herself, told on several speaking events and making her less mysterious, I want to present her live in perspective. I am picturing a four-year-old platinum blond perched in an olive tree overlooking her grandfather's olive farm and his Mount Whitney Olive Company. The company's name changed later to the Lindsey Olive Company. The little girl is staring out over the valley with one thought in mind, *Daddy just told me that Mommy is not coming back.* The next day, in Sunday School, she is cutting out pictures of Jesus, asking Him why.

Twenty years pass, and she is seated in a nightclub, across the table from a playboy named Hugh who, in turn, is in a far-off gaze that seems to tell of a deep emptiness of something never found, either.

The scene changes to her staring into the face of a young actor named Douglas who brings her a single rose as a gesture of understanding that life is really hard, but he cares.

The next clip shows her looking into the blue eyes of the famous Hollywood reporter named Leo Guild. He exclaims, "I've seen all kinds of eyes come through Hollywood and written articles about the faraway look in Marilyn Monroe's eyes besides many more." That's when he asked if he could write about Polly.

One day, she found what she was looking for; to her surprise, it was the same One she spoke to in the Lindsey Sunday School class in 1952. When she found Jesus, she knew she had found love at last. She never forgot about the person in her life who left, her mom. The last she heard of her mom was that she was headed for Hollywood looking for something she probably never found.

To this day, Polly still looks for her mom. After a tiring search over many years, Polly saw me one day months after leaving, and her countenance had changed. She was clutching a tiny scrap of paper, tears rolling down her cheeks. The paper indicated her mom cared from the birth announcement that described Polly stating, "Priscilla is such a tiny little thing, and we have had to leave her so that she can get special care. Oh, how I long to hold her in my arms." Polly had made a new discovery, with new knowledge, and her eyes expressed it.

Why do ugly, bad things happen on cold, December nights? This was one of those nights, when a once wonderful relationship ended in a night flight. Shortly thereafter forgiveness became the mediating topic. As the Bible instructs us to forgive. Col 3:13 ". . . Be gentle and kind, ready to forgive. Remember Christ forgave you and you must forgive others." Forgiveness is not optional in the Kingdom of God. Lingering memories of offenses is permissible to those offended but to God he erases even the memory of the sin if you truly repent. I knew that   repenting brought change and change would put a person on the right road. God only knows the true heart of a matter.

Still, Polly's two daughters and an old friend from the past will be more than willing to share, "Neither death, nor life, nor angels, nor principalities, nor things present, nor things to come will ever be able to separate you from Jesus that lives in you and us . . ."

On Christmas morning in 1999, Suzie, Kelly, Aaron, and I gathered to open stocking gifts. There was still a message left on the answering machine from the night before. It had been a year since we had seen Polly. We sat is silence as we listened to a humbled, broken voice accompanied by tears. Through this message the word "forgive" stood out, as it was mentioned eight times. The message ended with a beep and then silence after wishing us New Year's blessings. The silence was broken when Suzie began to cry. Shortly, Suzie returned to the Christmas fun.

Tears inside me welled up as I wondered about Suzie's thoughts and questions. I pondered if her thoughts held the same question that Polly had as a four year old wondering if Mommy was coming back, asking Jesus about all this. *How would Suzie handle this?*, I wondered.

With the wonders of unanswered questions and pain that must be pervading Suzie's mind I thought, *What about the restoration of forgiveness?* Yes, the key was restoration, through forgiveness.

My thoughts branched out to the millions of broken homes across America with children who were left motherless or fatherless. I went on to contemplate the thousands of gangs and their members who needed one or both parents' attention for guidance. Then I reflected on the Vietnam vets roaming the streets as homeless, because they didn't know how to forgive their government for sending them off to fight in a senseless war, by repeated futile orders.

Forgiveness of God brought me back to the reality of the moment and the healing promised if only forgiveness became the priority. The Bible passage from Colossians 3:13 reminded me, "Be gentle and ready to forgive; never hold grudges. Remember, the Lord forgave you, so you must forgive others." Forgiveness becomes my weapon, now. I have decided to forgive anyone in the past who has hurt me—and that's a big dish of forgiveness.

When you have been wronged and are wrestling with forgiveness, it seems like a tiger is on your back. How can one maneuver to the top, to pin this cat. If you can't get the upper hand in the situation, it's like stepping on a Vietnam land mine and never making it home. Forgiveness always has its challenges.

The secret of forgiveness is *choosing* to forgive, taking the first step yourself to a healing situation. The quickest remedy is the most difficult to surrender. The weapon of God's forgiveness is the one remedy to peace and the boomerang of exodus to the reentry of a relationship.

Hurting people can't hide in public or in the Army. I have met many who hurt. Usually, the hurting become the easiest targets for ridicule. One such person might easily have cracked up with the mean teasing from his peers and the ridicule from his drill sergeant in every way possible. How this guy made it after orders to rub his face into Nestles Crunch bars that he had hidden in his bunk bed was a mystery to me. Wiping his face back and forth, the sergeant reminded him of each of his weaknesses and unusual features, while yelling in his face. At least he didn't lose his face like some good-looking guys who entered Nam. Some guys lost limbs, others eyes, yet others their minds, and there were those who were burned beyond recognition. Some overcame these things; others didn't.

Hurting comes in all flavors, like the time I was 19 years old and entered the Laguna Beach Art Associations annual art contest, with thousands of other entrants. The big award was the coveted purchase prize. For any artist, this was a big deal to even be accepted into the show.

Hopes were high as I enthusiastically entered my favorite painting for consideration. My hurt came when I received the postcard back stamped, "Rejected." Hope didn't fade from that rejection because I didn't give up. Ten years later I tried out the same routine, again, but with a different painting. This time, my painting was accepted through a kind letter of acceptance. I was elated!

Another official letter came after that. My heart pounded in tearing it open and the words read, "Congratulations! Your painting titled, 'The Rapture' has been chosen as the purchase prize award." Time for skipping with joy, once more.

Pushing the button for a higher floor of my elevator ride seemed to be a good idea for a lift. The elevator was going down and taking me to an undesired floor, however. My instructor at USC, Keith Crown, was formerly a combat artist in the World War II Pacific

Arena. He looked at my drawing of a nude model, stared at it for a minute or two and bluntly said, "You can't draw!" His next utterance was, "Have you considered some other kind of interest, here, at USC?" Being dumped on the floor by his statement, I reassessed the art for myself, taking a second evaluation. I began thinking that the model looked more like a glorified stick drawing than I previously thought. I was becoming convinced that maybe I couldn't draw and that the instructor was right. Then I thought, *I know I can draw, though; maybe I'm having a bad drawing day.*

Deciding to prove him wrong, I returned with pencils sharpened, ready for war. I fought for the highest floor on the elevator, and I won. In fact, I won the Francis DeEridely award for the Best Freshman Drawing Student. The following three years produced more awards, but I won the Steinman Award for the Most Outstanding Painting Student. I'm glad I didn't stay with the prepunched elevator button of destiny that told me I couldn't draw; otherwise I never would have taken my own ride to the floor of combat artist as he had been.

Now, looking back on all the elevator ups and downs in my life, I think God doesn't interfere with the buttons of life that we push—even though we end up on impossible floors or no floor at all. If we do our part first by focusing on God's floor and let Him shift the gears for us, our weaknesses will fade as we stand on the platform of God's promise that "through God, all things are possible." We can arrive at the right floor every time and become winners in every situation.

The fifth, and final, reason I wrote this book is that I want to be wise. I want to be wise in answering God's call to be involved in His work, as He admonishes. The Bible says, "He who wins souls is wise." I want to be certain that I do not ignore the needs of people, needs they may not even be aware of until they, too, have the chance to know what the Bible says. In the words of Jesus, "With all the earnestness I possess I tell you this, unless you are born again you will not see the Kingdom of God." I truly want to be a partner with Jesus to bring glory to His name while I'm here, on earth.

As I understand what the Bible says, I read its meaning . . . with all the earnestness I, Ed Bowen, possess, unless I accept and believe in Jesus, I will be lost, for sure. I want to warn everyone I can since I consider this the truth in warnings.

In Basic Training, when we were warned by our drill sergeant about the real enemy, we not only were warned, but trained to be prepared as well. Preparation is vital in all events, but this event is a life-saving one. The solid ground of preparation has been laid out already, prepared by Jesus, the only One through whom you can have salvation. It's a decision that you, and you, alone, can make for yourself.

Those mentioned in this book, for the most part, are people who have, in earnest, made a commitment to Christ. Yet, I wonder about others whose paths I've crossed, as well as hundreds of people I've met and yet to meet.

Through my experiences, I hope others will be curious enough to question the reality of the Bible and the truth it holds. Maybe I have prompted questions in the reader, right now. If so, I would ask, "If you died today, where would you go?" Either of the following answers would be perilous:

1. I really don't know where I would go, but I'm a pretty good person and I've given life my best shot. So, if there is a God and a heaven, surely I'll make it there.

2. I'm too wretched a person, and surely God wouldn't let me enter heaven.

Either response is a sure loser. No one is worthy of making it to heaven. That is why Jesus came, to make us worthy. He wants to welcome everyone there, and He is the only ticket to heaven. To get there, the ticket must be received by asking Jesus into your heart. When this question is asked and the ticket is received, God will then see you as perfect. At the end of life, heaven will receive you. Without that ticket, heaven will not be your next home.

Chapter Twenty-Eight

The Art of Fishing

The combat artist team was a great bunch of guys. I loved being with them. We worked so well together and helped each other with artist tips. Out team consisted of six, including our civilian advisor. All of us, Vic, Tom, Roman, Jim, Fred, and I had completely different styles of artwork. Jim was the watercolorist who rendered as many as three great paintings each day. Vic (Victory Von Reynolds) worked on large canvases and painted in the old classic realism style. Roman drew a lot; he drew one picture that I loved so much that I kept his reference photo and 30 years later I am using it to paint one of the pictures in this book. Tom took thousands of photos just to get 10 or so real great ones and had his own great paintings. Tom was kind of shy, hiding his masterpieces from our sight. He appears as the guy in the coke painting, in the background, looking off into space.

As for me, I both drew and painted. I did many, many drawings in Vietnam, but chose to save the painting for Hawaii. I enjoyed my drawings very much but was never quite satisfied with my paintings. The non-quitter as I am, I attacked the painting thing and came up with the series in this book.

All of our artwork went to the Army war art collection, and we were told that the best stuff ended up in the Smithsonian, in Washington, DC. Some of our art went on the art tour. Later, I heard that it wasn't popular, because the Vietnam war wasn't popular.

I never saw three of the combat artists again; but Vic, the only non-officer in our group, except for me, showed up at my doorstep with his new art about three years later. He was painting clocks—truly great ones, and they became collectors items. One of them resembled the artwork of Toulouse La Trec. Vic brought his wife and her gorgeous 20-year-old sister, Jenny Gale, to the doorstep of our apartment (the Lanai Apartments in South Pasadena, California.)

The Lanai Apartments were another whole story altogether. It seemed to be the base of commitments of one kind or another. It turned out that matchmaking was one of the draws of this address. Mate-meeting just happened from this locale.

How did Dennis and Ed meet their mates? We could call it the art of fishing or fishing for the artist, or the art of hooking—with a line, of course. Here Dennis and I were at the same place we had so badly bungled the chair-fixing assignment when 14 people all landed on the floor. Just a close mile away from this camp we had our poles out dangling in the water. One line gets jerked, then tugged, and a 10-minute battle pursued, The monstrous, dark shadow of an object appears, seeming to dwarf our rowboat. The eyes of this brown giant appeared—the object motionless. We gasped in disbelief, stunned by this gigantic cod fish. Suddenly, a gaff was thrust down for a perfect hit, but missed, and the evidence slowly drifted out of sight. The big one got away. This *is* a true story, but no one believed us.

We had our strategy for fishing all worked out as to the place and position next to an island with an austere "No Trespassing" sign posted. We were rearing to go this one day.

We rowed swiftly and precisely to the place where the old-timers knew the big one was, hiding out. Nearing the large overhanging branches of tree, "Captain" Dennis quickly grabbed one of the branches to help us dock. All of a sudden, the boat took to sea and the feet of "the Captain" clung stubbornly to the stern, while his hands kept grasping the tree branch.

From ashore, the old-timers kept staring at this pseudo human bridge. I snickered as I fought to save him, but the oars got tangled in the tackle. The next thing I knew he was a screaming drill sergeant expounding on the heightened emotions until the screaming bridge was silenced by the murky waters of the big one's home. The drill sergeant surfaced with more expletives, and the belly laughs began. We couldn't contain it. Besides catching a cold over the sport, he spotted the big one. We knew we had to have him, no question about it. He seemed bigger than ever now. We did have him!

Something was different about the big one this time. The big one surfaced, out in the open, for an easy catch. The big one's eyes seemed to tell me that after years of hide and seek and outsmarting them all, he got tired of it all and up and died. Would you believe, he died *before* we caught him. Sizing up the big one and the situation, Dennis commented that we really should take him home to give him the burial he deserved. He wanted those proof photos to take first, to the amazement of future generations.

Ten years later, there were Dennis, Dave, and I rooming together at the Lanai Apartments. This time, however, the fishing wasn't for fish but for gals. Ever since Riverside, as boys, we were always fishing for the best one. But, who wasn't? We had just finished reading *The Right Man, Right Woman* book. Dennis and I concluded that we didn't need to be tricky fishermen in trying to catch the right lady. We decided to follow God's instructions of waiting and watching. We were at a different fishing hole, without a line or a pole, just waiting. Then Saturday came.

It was obvious that the "fish" weren't biting this day, particularly since Dennis and I were engrossed in a football game. Dennis had one eye on the game and the other eye on his own game, a man-eating piranha. The piranha was entertaining Dennis while gulping on whole, live gold fish, one at a time. Game time was interrupted by footsteps on our porch.

Getting a glimpse of a shapely shadow through the half-closed blinds, we discovered a girl standing there. Our friend, Bob, had written her, and she was responding by coming through a 1,500-mile trek to make connection with him at our place. Bob never showed. By this time, he was well on his way to Vietnam.

After her knock, I encouraged Dennis to answer, since he was closer. When the door was open, we saw a real beauty before our eyes. She stood there, speechless, and he, frozen. I decided it was time for my exit and left them mumbling some nonsense to each other. Dennis's dish of rocky road got abandoned for another "dish" where the road wasn't rocky, but moved. Trying to involve myself with a different scene, I spotted an enormous pink Cadillac with a New Mexico license plate hogging a couple of parking spaces. I knew, by then, that Dennis' fishing days were over. I don't know who caught who. This "fish" didn't get away. Three months later, Pastor Chuck Smith was inviting Dennis to kiss his bride. As best man, I told myself, "So this is what happens when a waiting mole kissed the fish that didn't get away."

My fishing days were not yet over, nor were Dave's. While I went on my solo fishing trip, Dave headed south to San Diego, to Marlin waters. Dave disappeared for 20 years or so, until I found myself biting my tongue eating ice cream and watching television. Suddenly, there was Dave, the big one, who almost got away. Shock and excitement filled his face as the newscaster asked him, "How does it feel to be fished out of the sea as your burning boat was sinking?" This time, Dave was the big one who was three miles off the La Jolla shores. Dave's fishing sense has turned to banking cents, now, as his career is banking.

On a scale of one to ten, mine was the best catch! Fifteen years from the first time I cast my line, I got the bite.

I was at my jewelry shop in San Diego, when a beautiful little blue-eyed, seven-year-old girl came with her aunt and my friend, Bob, to visit for the day. Later, the little girl's aunt asked if I would join them in a Mother's Day dinner she was having for her family. I accepted!

I got in the car, and after 100 miles, I was looking into the most beautiful face I had ever seen. Polly was her name, the mommy of seven-year-old, Kelley. The next minute I began gazing out the apartment window to think about what I had just seen. In doing so, something so memorable invaded my thoughts. I remembered the commitment to God I had made from a spot not more than 20 yards away to the Lanai Apartment balcony with my fishing buddy,

Dennis the Mole. The commitment was to wait for the right woman—a promise to God.

When I realized that was the very balcony of commitment, I knew I had come full circle to the one for me. I thought, *Remember all those many years ago when I read the book "Right Man, Right Woman" and I committed to God that I would wait for Him to bring his choice to me? Remember that very porch? Now God has completed His part of the deal because I waited. It was worth the wait, wasn't it?* I thought, *Yes.* Several months later, Polly and I were taking our marriage vows under a large oak tree.

In 1997, over two years ago, after 15 years of marriage, it ended. This does not mean, however, that God doesn't have another plan to replace my broken one. After my disaster, God will heal with another answer—always a surprise to me.

Chapter Twenty-Nine

More Surprises

Just when life seems to humming along, another surprise brings a wake-up call. The surprise of opportunity laid at my feet gives me new excitement, particularly in a place I call Miracle Mountain.

Miracle Mountain is a work haven for happy "elves" to accomplish honorable work. The "elves" of Miracle Mountain are no different from you and me, but their former professions were different. Drug dealings, embezzlement, con-artistry, caused them to become prisoners of life, in prison. Freedom took them on a path to Miracle Mountain where their creativity is no longer used for selfish purposes to a rotten end, but eternal purposes, now. In this haven it doesn't seem like work because busy hands and minds are creating Christian Jewelry for an outreach.

An average days begins with prayer and Bible study. As I sit at the end of the table before work, I look out at the often snow-capped Miracle Mountain. Then, I turn my focus to Tony, a Messianic Jew, who is always smiling and has a happy beat in his heart. The next person is Terry, a real hero to the Carnegie Institute because of saving a lady's life from fire recently. Before, Terry was involved in various drug activities. He is one of the most sincere Christian believers I've known for years—a kind soul. Kim also sits at our table, but was formerly involved with meth and heroin habit. She was formerly incarcerated. Wendy, well-educated and very gifted, used to be a hippie in search for whatever and found Jesus in the process. Her two children, Miranda a Christian filled with hope and her brother, Andy, the campus guy for the younger coeds, is loving the Lord with all his heart, too.

Charlie sits at the other end of the table from me. Charlie is one special guy, all right! Charlie Parker had one of the best drug rings going for a long time, which finally ended him in prison. Going back in time, Charlie was also a Charley killer in Vietnam. This Charlie did a good tour in Nam, however, and lived to prove it. Vietnam prepared him for drug trafficking, later. Fear didn't daunt him, however, as he entered the drug world. After a bit, he came to a point of no return that landed him in jail, for quite a while. Now rather than serving master time, he serves the Master of all time. When Charlie prays, things happen—all for the better, every time. Charlie is one of the most creative people in the shop for bottle captions. He knows the Scriptures, which come to him easily as he ponders a new phrase for one of the caps. Miracle Mountain continues to honor the Lord in music and word each day.

We work for happiness, the happiness of people because each of us knows what hopeless and despair is. The freedom from fear of death in Vietnam to me is something to be cherished. The freedom from the drug world is priceless to Charlie. The freedom from the evils of bondage and rescue that ensued are all special to the others in the shop. We were all rescued from the darkness of evil ways and life patterns. And, we are no more special than anyone else in this world. So Miracle Mountain is just the right name for the shop.

As I look at Henrietta Mears' Miracle Mountain, Mt. San Bernardino, we have our own Miracle Mountain at its base. We are dreaming big as she did, as explained in the book about her— *Dream Big*. So many people's lives have been touched by the place she called Miracle Mountain. One of the most well-known people was Billy Graham, when he came to a crossroad in his own hour of decision as a young man, right there at Miracle Mountain.

Chapter Thirty

Why Cover Up?
The Good, the Bad and the Ugly

I was a cover up artist, even before I became an artist. What about you? What did I cover up today? My cover up is not as costly as some are, though. What do some attorneys cover up—lots, and at who's expense? What do criminals cover up? Plenty. What does the military cover up, camouflage? That's another story. What does a small child cover up from his parent(s). What does a teacher cover up when he's in a pickle for an answer? What does the speeder try to cover up with police? How many cover ups go on each day?

One of the good cover ups is the make-up thing, like *Cover Girl*. For the good of women, make-up improves the looks. Another good cover up is sensitivity to someone's feelings. In my divorce situation, cover up was essential. But I didn't cover up my terrified feelings of being in the wrong military school. I had to *open* up to my superiors. There was a payoff to the open-up in this case. I'm here to tell it.

The bad cover up is like the time my clinic mate thought I needed the needle. He got it, however, when I needled him first. Then, I got it after all, later.

What could be uglier than having your face covered up with Nestles Crunch from orders by a superior. What was the purpose anyway? A face full of chocolate didn't cover up the ugly emotion of the sergeant or the homeliness of the one being demeaned. Yet, these all keep us in bondage.

Did the cover up of drugs bring freedom? So, what does cover-up really accomplish? It's better not to be in camouflage.

The better part of cover up that I experienced was hiding my weaknesses from public eye and scrutiny. Why not? It wasn't hurting any one else. For sanity, I covered up the learning thing in helicopter school and clerk school so I could survive each military day. If I hadn't covered up these things in the military, I surely would have been dead by now.

In teaching, the holes in my teaching awareness needed cover up, or my survival in the classroom of students would have been fatal. But the school newspaper of Villa Park High School showed my capability—I must have been a cover up artist.

Villa Park still looks the same, and today's students are just as interested as the ones I taught 33 years ago, particularly about Vietnam. I stopped by there recently, and found an enthusiastic group of teenagers wanting to know more about Vietnam. We have a date in one week to look at slides together, in the very room I taught—amazing!

Going down the San Diego Freeway I pass the off-ramp that takes me to Fountain Valley High School. Driving into this community I find the landscape the same as before. At present, the high school is filled with Vietnamese students eating lunch on surfer hill, where the gospel was shared before. How ironic is that?

Now, though, the people have changed. It makes me wonder where I am. More than 30 years ago I was in the confines of Vietnam by order. Now, free and home again, I look into the faces of the Vietnamese in Little Saigon, near Huntington Beach, California. The place has changed for these people and so has their desire to be in their old home of communism, thousands of miles from here. Freedom is their greatest desire, now. Only recently, this community had a gigantic uprising against one man of their own who wanted the North Vietnam flag of Viet Cong posted for all to see. They called this treason. His demise became uncertain, as he was pounded by the majority in the community for his treasonous display. The war did do something; eventually it brought freedom to the captives from both sides.

Out of the army, now, I am reminded of the freedom I have from everything connected to war. My war years continue as a Christian soldier. This is the army I have enlisted in, and I ask my Commander, God, what He wants to do with me, anything He wants. I am ready for duty, ready to die, ready to share, ready for the situation of His moment. I am ready to march onward as I sing His tune of "Give Me your heart, give Me your life, now go with your left, right, left, right into His kingdom. I won't go AWOL, take a permanent leave, or look to my right and then my left, but stay on the straight and narrow path, with His help. I have the spark of His life. Thank You, Sir, for not sending me to the place where everyone draws fire, forever! Amen!"

Credits

John Anderson—Although I'm sure he forgot me, I never forgot him. He was my camp counselor in 1960, who prayed with me as I accepted Christ as my Savior. He prayed first, and then waited for me. I froze in fear and silence for quite a while. Then, out came the shortest prayer he had probably ever heard. It was, "Christ, come in." That was it; and off I went, with him shaking his head and wondering what I was all about. But I was serious because I had just heard one week of talks by Tom Bade—a young man who knew how to tell about the gospel story like few have ever heard it.

Mom—She was also my Sunday School teacher who sowed seeds in both the Word and example.

Dad—His example of integrity made me want to follow in his footsteps.

Great Grandmother Summerbell—She prayed for her future generation grandchildren: my sister and me, and my co-author cousin, Camilla, being three of them.

Polly, my former wife—She showed me what prayer and Bible-reading were all about. Her display of compassion toward the hurting was always an example to me.

Aunt Eileen—(actually Polly's aunt) She gave me great encouragement by giving me her inputs on my paintings. She is also an artist and knows how to give a good critique. When she read my rough draft, she really became excited and told me she thought I had a best seller. Her best encouragement was telling me to go forward with full speed ahead, while the book is hot; so I did.

Nathan Miller—He is a USC cinema major who critiqued the rough draft. He helped me broaden my story with more details for deeper interest.

Bill and Barbara Peters—They both were instrumental in supporting my efforts in prayer and counsel. Also a Vietnam vet, Bill was one I consider a real hero who spent time in the Marines. He wrote a book *First Force Recon—Sunrise at Midnight*. I painted a series of paintings for him while he worked on his book.

Chuck Dean—He encouraged me in going forward with the book and gave me the title, *Drawing Fire*. By the way, he was a drill sergeant when I was at Fort Ord—in the adjacent camp to mine during Basic Training. I didn't know him then. He also authored *Nam Vet*.

Billy Graham—He told the message of the cross, without tampering with the exactness of its reality. He preached the gospel of the cross at Miracle Mountain in 1967, just prior to my Vietnam experience.

Bill Bright and the Campus Crusade messengers, Dick Edict, and Marshall Foster—They all took time to sew the Word into me. Marshall was at the Young Life Camp in British Columbia when I made my decision.

Bob Myers—He was my best man. Bob was always there with an ear and a timely word when I needed it the most.

Keith Baylor—He was a Young Life high school leader who was instrumental in leading me on the path to Christianity.

Don Williams—He is a Hollywood Presbyterian college department pastor. Don nurtured my Christian faith while I was at USC.

Ed Trenner—He was a Youth for Christ leader who taught me how to lead Campus Life meetings.

Ray Smith—Ray was a UCLA football star who took afternoons to teach Dennis and me how to study the Bible.

Hal Lindsey—He took a bunch of us under his wing at the Jesus Christ Light and Power House at UCLA. He taught us the basics of the prophecy, about spiritual warfare, and how our daily life with Christ should be.

Camilla (Joy) Young—She is a former technical editor at the Jet Propulsion Laboratory in Pasadena, California. She is my cousin, qualified in writing and editing. Her strength was in helping me to say what I felt and to describe the exactness of situations I had experienced without distorting any of my material. She has known me from the time I was a little guy, from day one in America. She met me for the first time when I was skipping in my dirt driveway in Santa Barbara. We lived in the garage while building our home, then.

GOD—I am most of all grateful for God who is, indeed, the inspiration I carry with me in everything I do today. And I am grateful for all the people He allowed me to meet on this path of faith.

To order additional copies of

Drawing Fire

Have your credit card ready and call

(877) 421-READ (7323)

or send $10.95 each + $4.95* S&H to

WinePress Publishing
PO Box 428
Enumclaw, WA 98022

*add $1.00 S&H for each additional book ordered